Acknowledgements

The Anderson daughters, Chris Kwong, Carla Benjamin, and Kate Canady, grandchildren Laura and Alan Kwong

Cover Design & Art Work by Carla Benjamin

Printed at Bang Printing, Brainerd, MN

Marketing and fulfillment assistance by: The Brainerd Dispatch, Brainerd, MN

Research assistance by The Brainerd Public Library, Echo Publishing Co., Pequot Lakes, MN, Joan Wiesner, and Les Sellnow, Brainerd Daily Dispatch editor 1974-1984

Transcription by Kathy Zak, Brainerd, MN

Published by

EVERGREEN PRESS
OF BRAINERD, LLC

201 West Laurel St., Brainerd, MN 56401
(218) 828-6424

ISBN#: 978-0-9755252-9-6

Introduction

Hal Anderson was gifted with the ability to see, feel and express what to many was overlooked as being commonplace in nature. His thoughts and feelings were shared with literally thousands of people through his column, "Hiking with Hal," which was published for 35 years in the Brainerd Daily Dispatch.

The columns resulted in a legion of fans who looked forward to his musings in The Dispatch each Sunday. They were low-key columns. No beating of the drum for special causes, no vitriolic diatribes against anyone or anything; just thoughts and observations about nature and the animals and plants that are a part of it. The columns were like a chat with a friendly neighbor over the backyard fence.

Yet, the columns conveyed a subtle, but clear message—the beauty and wonder of nature is all about us, but if it is to be preserved and appreciated in the future, we must be good stewards today.

The columns were as varied as Hal's experiences in nature. Sighting a deer or a hawk on the wing might be the stimulus for that week's column, or a stroll in the woods with his Golden Retriever might bring forth his appreciation for a good canine companion. Or, experiences with a new pup that had a penchant for escaping confinement could stimulate a column about the trials and tribulations of getting that canine companion through the puppy stages.

Whatever the subject matter, the approach was always calm, reasoned and congenial. That was Hal. To know him was to like him. With his ruddy Scandinavian complexion, crewcut and ever-present smile, he brightened whatever gathering he graced with his presence. At Exchange Club, he often led the group in song with his powerful voice. "Come on everybody, join in and sing," he would urge. "If you can't sing good, sing loud." One could easily believe that the word congenial was coined to describe Hal.

It was a weekly day brightener when he'd stop by the newsroom to drop off his column during the years I served as managing editor and then editor, something he most often did in person, rather than use the postal service. He was perceptive. If I was busy, he'd proffer that trademark, smiling, "Howdy," hand me the column and leave. On other occasions, when the pressure was off, he might pull up a chair and we'd kick back and chat.

The columns very seldom required editing. The prose was clear, straight-forward and unadorned.

Though neither of us knew it at the time, Hal played a key role in launching me on a second career. The editor of The Farmer magazine asked him to write a column on horses. During one of our visits, he said, "I told him I didn't know all that much about horses, but that you do and you should be the one to write the column." Based on Hal's recommendation, the magazine editor contacted me and the rest is history. Ultimately, I left the newspaper profession and have gone on to write for equine magazines and author books about matters equine. Hal was both happy and proud that he was instrumental in getting me started with The Farmer. It was a part of his totally unselfish nature.

Hal was the consummate family man. It was obvious that his wife, Doris, was the love of his life and that their daughters were his pride and joy.

It would have been a distinct loss if the columns written by Hal had slipped away and faded from memory, buried in a newspaper's files. Thanks to Doris and her daughters, with the help of others, that isn't going to happen. A collection of Hal's columns are presented in this book. It is a fitting tribute to a fine man and a dedicated conservationist, as well as being a treat for all who read these pages.

Enjoy.

Les Sellnow

Table of Contents

Table of Contents

Winter

Winter doesn't begin officially until the solstice on December 22, but the reality almost always arrives ahead of the calendar's schedule. With the ground completely covered in snow and most of the lakes ice-bound, winter weather has definitely begun.

The first snowfall is always welcome, though the enthusiasm with which it is received depends on our age and frame of mind. Children are delighted by new snow. Most adults would like to greet it with the same reckless abandon, except that we know too much. We see the beauty of a snow-covered landscape and we have the feeling that we are going to tire of it during the next five months. One part of ourselves admires the Christmas-card scene, while another part reminds us that we will be spending nearly half the year in a world covered with ice and snow.

Falling snowflakes have a special beauty that is almost as hypnotic as watching the dancing flames of a blazing hearth fire. The constant movement and shifting patterns of both can fill us with a sense of contentment and peace. The house that we moved out of a few years ago had a pair of floodlights mounted under the eaves. Sometimes on a snowy night, we used to turn on these lights and sit in the dark living room entranced by the snowfall.

Sometimes it seems as though the weather forecasts tend to increase anxiety. We are warned well in advance of every winter storm. If we plan to travel, the advanced warning is good to have. On the other hand we often spend four or five days worrying about an approaching storm that never arrives.

Outdoor work too can be hampered by the weather. I find most times that working outside in winter usually isn't as bad as I thought it was going to be. With proper clothing one can work outside in relative comfort in all but the most severe conditions. Some things can be delayed if the weather is really bad. Such postponements can have two dramatically different effects, depending on how we look at them. We may feel completely frustrated by having to change our plans, spending a day or two fretting over something that can't be helped. On the other hand we may find ourselves in for a relaxing period of unplanned time that we can choose to enjoy in any way we desire. A north country winter can be really enjoyable if we take it one day at a time!

December Is...

It's hard to predict what the new year will bring, but we can be fairly certain about some of the things we will encounter in December.

December will bring the latest sunrises, the earliest sunsets, and long nights for restful sleep. It will bring us blizzard winds howling around the eaves and whistling in the chimney. It will bring us the chance for a relaxing evening in front of a hearth fire with a big bowl of popcorn. December is snowflakes sifting down through the dusk and the rasping sound of shovels on concrete walks. It is cold, so cold that the snow squeaks when we walk on it. Sometimes December is an early "January thaw" and sometimes freezing rain that covers our world in a crystal coating of ice. December is a careful man shoveling or raking snow off the roof.

December means an extra serving of seeds in the bird feeder. It means delicate tiny pine siskins and big greedy grosbeaks. It means grouse feeding in the aspen tops when the lower bushes are buried in snow. It is owls hooting softly in the evening twilight and coyotes singing over moonlit white hills.

December is school kids and teachers both hoping for a "Snow Day," and dreaming of Christmas vacation. It is skiing and skating and snowmobiling, snowmen, snow forts and snowball fights. It is cross-country skis that won't go cross country unless there is a packed trail—and snowshoes that will.

December brings sleigh bells, church bells, and charity bells, all ringing out with joy. It brings Christmas trees, wreaths and mistletoe. It brings Christmas cards to be addressed and notes to write to those special people that we send greetings to at least once each year. It brings a new tie for dad and some jewelry for mom...and what can we get for Aunt Helen? December is mothers wrapping gifts after the kids are in bed and kids shaking, squeezing, and figuring out all the presents before they are opened.

December in the north country is certainly lutefisk and lefse, nuts, candy, cookies, and mince pie. It is rosettes, krumkake, fatigman, and hot fruit soup. It is family gatherings and singing the old familiar carols at candlelit church services, and opening presents around the tree. December is many things...most of them very good.

Let's go for a snowshoe hike. It will be more strenuous than our summer outings, but it will give us a chance to see things that we couldn't any other way.

Our daughter Carla talked me into going through the snowy woods to begin the new year. My snowshoes hadn't been used for nearly two years, but they had a familiar feeling once I had strapped them on and walked a few yards. The snow was deep and fluffy, and even with the webs, we sank about six inches. It wasn't easy walking, but part of our reason for going out was to get some exercise.

The trees were frost-covered when we started out, the sun had burned through the morning fog, and the whole world seemed to be sparkling. The sky was a deep, almost spring-like blue. It was a glorious day to be outside! A few yards from the house we began to notice tracks in the snow. Rabbits and squirrels had been moving about in spite of the deep snow. In a number of places we could see where a squirrel had leaped from a tree branch into the deep snow and then laboriously jumped its way back to a tree trunk.

Down below the hill we were impressed by the numerous little tracks made by mice and other small rodents. One trail ended abruptly with the tragic story clearly told in the snow prints. A small hawk, perhaps a kestrel, had dived on a mouse, leaving its wing prints in the snow as it took off with its prey.

Near the edge of the woods a hole in the snow with no tracks leading up to it attracted our attention. Tail and wing prints showed that a ruffed grouse had burrowed into the snow and had later taken flight from its insulated bed. A bit farther down the trail we found imprints left by a short-tailed weasel. At each jump it had left clear marks of feet, a long slim body, and a short tail. We went by the old spring-fed stock-watering pond, finding it almost completely free of ice in spite of the frigid weather we endured the week before. Down near the pond we came upon some very fresh tracks made by a fast-moving animal. The powdery snow held no clear footprints, but the tracks might have been made by a running coyote. There appeared to be too much disturbed snow for the prints to have been made by a deer. We followed the trail for a while and discovered that it divided into two deer tracks. The supposed "coyote" trail had been made by two deer running in the same tracks.

We circled out of the woods into the young tree plantation, finding the traveling even harder there. The snow surface was crusted but not strong enough to support our weight. We broke through at every step, raising our snowshoes straight up to prevent the toes from catching under the edge of the crust. Out in the open we found many more tracks made by small seed-eating birds. Little birds visited every weed that protruded above the snow. As we headed back toward the house, we sighted a rare, large bird. A pileated woodpecker went swooping by in front of us. The big woodpecker was the only remarkable wildlife we saw, but we had enjoyed reading the story of many other birds and animals in the white tracks left in the snow.

Wood Heat

There was a time when almost everyone heated homes by burning wood. Rising standards of living, along with cheap gas and heating oil, caused most families to switch to the more easily controlled fossil fuels. A few years ago high-priced petroleum led a number of folks, especially in rural areas, to return to the fuel used by their ancestors.

Our home has the best of both worlds—a thermostatically controlled combination wood/oil furnace. We had been burning oil all fall until early last week. The oil fire is easier to control in mild winter weather. Wood fires, burning at low levels, tend to allow the accumulation of creosote in the chimney, making frequent cleaning a necessity. The real economy of firing with wood comes during our coldest weather.

We were waiting patiently for our winter's supply of firewood to be delivered with only about a half-cord of wood left. We had ordered five cords from a neighbor who didn't have time to deliver it until after the deer hunting season. The wood, when delivered, was well seasoned, but had absorbed some moisture from our early snowfall. Our son-in-law Gary and grandsons Alan and Neal (ages four and six), who visited us at Thanksgiving, spent a considerable amount of time and energy putting some of the wood into our basement. We still had to wait a couple of weeks for it to be dry enough to burn well.

Firing with wood is more of an art than a science. Different species of wood burn at varying rates. The amount of moisture in the wood is always a concern. Even the size of the chunks is a factor for consideration. Small dry sticks are best for a quick hot fire. Birch is ideal in this situation; the paper-like bark ignites easily. Larger chunks are best for holding a fire overnight. Dense woods like oak or ash serve best for this purpose. Our new wood supply contains some ironwood, which is the densest wood that grows in this area.

I learned about firing with wood at an early age. The farmhouse in which I grew up was heated entirely with wood. We had two cast iron heating stoves and a wood-burning kitchen range. The farmhouse was not insulated, so it took a big woodpile to last us through the winter! Those wood stoves all had manually controlled draft openings and dampers. Frequent attention was required to prevent the fire from over-heating or going out. There is, of course, a certain amount of labor involved in heating with wood, but there is a good deal of cost savings too, even when we purchased our wood instead of cutting our own.

Most people who have lived with it agree that wood heat is a very comfortable kind. Even when the thermostat is not calling for heat, the wood fire burns at low flame to prevent its going out, producing a low, but steady, heat that keeps the house comfortable at all times until the wood is burned up.

Sixty-nine Christmas cards, each with a personal message, are in the mail, mostly due to long hours put in by Doris. Most of the presents are purchased –if not wrapped. The nine-foot Christmas tree is up and decorated. It's time now to make the fruit soup. What! You've never heard of fruit soup? It's an old Scandinavian treat that our family looks forward to every Christmas season.

I remember fruit soup that my grandmother used to make when I was a small boy on a central Minnesota farm. That was before electricity in rural areas so there was no refrigeration. The soup was, of necessity, made from dried fruits, mostly dried apples, raisins and prunes, served hot, usually as an appetizer before the lutefisk.

I had almost forgotten this old favorite when, several years ago, I saw a fruit soup recipe in a magazine. I gave it a try and the resulting product wasn't bad, but it didn't taste like Grandma's had! I made the soup only once each year, but experimented by adding and subtracting different fruits until I got something that looked and tasted close to Grandma's fruit soup. Even so, it isn't exactly the same. I use several kinds of fruit that were not available to Grandma. Still our immediate family has learned to love it.

My recipe isn't an exact one. It varies a bit from year-to-year, depending on what dried fruits are available—an opportunity for the cook to exercise a bit of creative expression. Here is the basic recipe:

'Da Fruit Soup:
1 C. pearl tapioca (soaked overnight in 4 C. water)
In a big pot cook the tapioca until it turns from white to clear.
Stir constantly over low heat or all the tapioca will stick to the bottom of the pot.
1 lb. mixed dried fruit, cut into jelly bean size pieces
1 small can white cherries
4 C. water
2 C. sugar
1/2 lemon, cut into small pieces (including rind)
1 stick cinnamon
1/2 lb. raisins
1/2 lb. currants
1 small can pineapple juice
1 orange, cut into small pieces (including rind)
8 whole cloves, tied in cheesecloth for removal before serving
1/2 bottle white port (or other sweet wine)
Simmer all these ingredients in the pot with the tapioca for two hours. Stir often.
Add wine near the end of cooking. (Grandma didn't use wine, but I think it adds something!)
Fruit soup should be served hot and can be reheated as often as necessary.

Christmas is a celebration little affected by the passing of time. Every so often they advertise some new songs and new toys, but the essence of the holiday remains the same. We listen to the ancient story of Christ's birth and sing the old carols. We gather with family and friends, exchanging familiar greetings. The spirit of loving and giving seems as fresh and new as ever.

My Christmas memories go back to a tree lit with real candles. I grew up in a rural area that had no electric power until I was twelve years old. The lighting of the tree in those days was a very special event. All the family moved into the front room where the tree had been set up. We attached candles to the branches with spring-clip candleholders. Father was the only one allowed to light the four-inch long candles. Everyone sat and admired the beauty of the tree for ten to fifteen minutes until the candles were extinguished for safety's sake

My father was the custodian of our little country church. Part of his job was to decorate and light the twenty-foot tall spruce tree that dominated the front of the church. To reach the tree's top he had a candle lighter and snuffer made from a bamboo fishing rod. The Christmas program took place in front of this magnificent tree, and each child who took part received a bag of peanuts and Christmas candy—ribbon candy and other hard candy along with filled raspberries and best of all, chocolate creams. We did have fudge and divinity made at home, but store-bought candy was a special treat. Some years we had a Christmas program at our country school too and we were blessed with an additional sack of candy and nuts!

My childhood home was a farm with wooded pasture. The only evergreens that grew there were a species of juniper we called Red Cedar. The cedar foliage was rather brown, not considered suitable for Christmas trees. Christmas trees had to be spruce or balsam fir, cut in the northern Minnesota swamps and imported especially for Christmas. It was not until we moved to the north country that we were able to go out and cut our own Christmas tree.

Sunrises and sunsets have been particularly attractive lately. One thing that I really like about this time of year is the opportunity to witness both the sun's rising and setting and still have time for a long night's sleep. We usually watch the sunrise while having breakfast at our kitchen table, which is set right against the bay window where we have a good view to the east and southeast. Oak, aspen and birch trees are scattered across that part of our yard, the bare branches and a few remaining oak leaves forming a dark tracery as the sunrise brightens beyond them.

Sunsets have a completely different feeling. We have a clear view of a large segment of the southwest sky. The tops of the pine trees on a distant ridge form a jagged silhouette below the lighted sky. Many of our evenings have had a few clouds in the west to add pattern and shades of color to the sunset. Each evening varies with colors ranging from pastel pink to flaming red.

Mild temperatures have brought us a bonus number of mornings with heavy frost accumulations causing really spectacular sunrises. The frost coats every twig on the hardwoods, lending them a feathery appearance. Then as the sun clears the horizon, the frost sparkles, like having the whole forest decorated in diamonds. I feel really rich on such mornings! As I go out our driveway on my way to work, the Christmas trees in the field all appear flocked with delicate white. Even the weeds along the road form beautiful winter bouquets with shining crystals on every leaf and flower.

On sunny afternoons the landscape loses its frosty covering and we see the tans and faded browns of late autumn once again. The scene is less spectacular than wind-sculpted snowdrifts, but I have the feeling that we will have plenty of time to enjoy snow before spring arrives! The uncovered foliage has another advantage too—it absorbs more solar heat than a snow-covered landscape. We can let the wood fire go out on those sunny afternoons and save our firewood for the colder weather yet to come.

Every year at this time we think about New Year's resolutions. The ones that I usually make never seem to last through the month, much less the year. This time I want to make some resolutions that will cause only minor changes in the way I live.

I am resolved to go out more often to enjoy winter. We used our snowshoes only once last winter and we should do more. I want to take time to see the graceful sculpture of wind-drifted snow and the purple shadows on sparkling snow. I want to hear the squeak of snow under my boots and have at least one winter picnic. I'll listen at night for the singing of coyotes and the hooting of owls. When severe cold keeps us indoors, I'll take time to enjoy a hearth fire and a bowl of popcorn.

When spring finally arrives, I want to go hiking along a creek where I can hear as well as see the water running free. I'll watch for ice-out on the lakes and sunlight flashing on the waves. I'll listen for the song of the first robin and the peeping of tree frogs. I'll appreciate the first blades of green grass and the pink haze of budding trees. I'll take time to search the sunny roadsides for wild strawberries, little ruby morsels that taste as sweet as my childhood memories of them.

On our summer hikes I'll stop to inhale the sweet fragrance of delicate wild rose blossoms. I want to spend more time fishing and feel the tug of a walleyed pike on my line. I want to hear the soft whistle of a mourning dove on a summer morning and end the day listening to a whippoorwill repeating its name. I'll listen to the happy sounds of children on a swimming beach and notice the rattle of June beetles' wings against the screen door on a warm night. I want to see thunderheads piling up in the west at the end of a hot day and listen to the soothing sound of rain on the roof.

I won't really need a resolution to get out and savor autumn's beauty. I will try to find time for some bird hunting, even though work on our Christmas tree plantation keeps us busy. Farley, our golden retriever, will forget all his training if we don't get him out to a place where he can flush a pheasant or grouse. I will find time for deer hunting. Unlikely as it sounds now, I'll even welcome the first snow if it improves hunting conditions.

A major sort of resolution that fits in with all of these others is a determination to slow down. Those of us who live in the country have many things of interest and beauty all around us. All we need to do at any season of the year is to stop and enjoy.

Frosty Windows

We had planned to take a hike on New Year's Day although the morning temperature of 35 below zero made the prospect rather unattractive! I went instead to my den, a second floor room with windows overlooking our lake. Here I can usually see enough of the world of nature to find some inspiration without going outside on a frigid day.

On that morning the storm windows were almost completely covered with opaque frost. The sight of those frosted windows brought back memories of my childhood on the farm. In those days we slept in unheated bedrooms without storm windows. Frost would often build up a quarter-inch thick on the glass. I expected to hear my father rattling the poker in the old cast iron stove as I waited for the comforting roar of a wood fire taking the chill out of our house.

The frost on my den windows wasn't very thick. Each of three windows had eight small panes of glass. Each of those panes was like a framed picture with intricate patterns etched in the glass. From a little distance some looked like delicate lace fans; others had finely-veined many-pointed patterns like celery leaves. Each was different from the others. A couple of them reminded me of aerial photos of river deltas, the mud banks white instead of black. The branched patterns looked like streams flowing through the flatlands at river's mouth. One pane resembled a photograph of a forest scene, two sturdy oaks growing in the foreground.

I grabbed my hand lens for a closer look. The sharp-pointed frost crystals along the edges of the panes were like a grove of spruce silhouetted against the sky on the top of a ridge. One small section made me think of a wooded point of land sticking out into a lake with the forest growth reflected in the water's surface.

Perhaps I should have gone outdoors and braved the elements to start the new year in a proper fashion. Maybe I indulge too much in fantasy as a means of avoiding the cold. Still the frost patterns were there to be seen and enjoyed.

The Barometer: Predictor of Change

The barometer rose sharply during the night and we knew before we looked at the thermometer that our hiking weather today would be clear and cold. A reading of twenty-six degrees below zero confirmed our estimate, and layered warm clothes were the order of the day. The thermometer and our senses told us it was cold; the barometer reading, high and rising, told us it would probably stay cold for awhile.

The barometer, a simple device for measuring changes in air pressure, is a useful invention for anyone who is affected by weather. Low or falling air pressure usually indicates the approach of a storm, while rising pressure brings clear weather. At this time of year, a low reading means snow and a high reading means cold.

The first barometers, invented in the seventeenth century, consisted of a glass tube about three feet long, closed at one end and filled with mercury. This tube was inverted in a dish of mercury, the air pressure supporting the column of mercury to a height of about thirty inches in the tube. Changes in air pressure caused a corresponding change in the height of the mercury column. This same principle is employed in the most accurate barometers used today.

One enterprising German, Otto von Guericke, invented a water barometer about the same time. Since water is much lighter than mercury, the tube for this barometer had to be thirty-four feet high! Von Guericke fastened the tube to the side of his house with the bottom end in a tub of water. He floated a little carved wooden man in the top of the column, the figure going up in good weather and down in bad. The neighbors thought it was magic. Von Guericke's little wooden mannequin was probably the first weather man in history!

Most modern barometers are of the aneroid or dry type. These measure changes in pressure using a small metal bellows from which most of the air has been removed. The bellows is linked to a needle on a dial, which moves the pointer to indicate the pressure changes. These are not as accurate as the liquid type, but since the smallest mercury barometer is about three feet high, the dry type is much easier to transport and use.

Even an inexpensive aneroid barometer, though not truly scientifically accurate, will show relative changes in air pressure. It can tell us whether to plug in the engine heater on the car or get out the snow shovel. In summer it can indicate whether we should plan a picnic or tell the kids to put their bikes away before it rains. Barometers are even useful for indicating when the fish will bite best!

Our hiking has been limited by extremely cold weather. Even the morning hike to the garage to start the cars has become an unpleasant chore. When we first step out the door from a warm house, the weather seems invigorating. The squeak of snow underfoot tells us the temperature is well below zero, but it takes a few minutes for the cold to penetrate. When the northwest wind comes sweeping around the corner, driving the cold into our bodies with vindictive force, all the joy goes out of winter.

The temperature may only be 12 degrees below zero but the wind chill makes it feel like 40 below. I'm not sure about the weather bureau broadcasting the wind chill factor. It's bad enough to go out on a subzero morning without knowing about that deadly wind waiting to impale us. It's a mistake, I suppose, to call the cold vindictive. Vindictive implies a spirit of revenge, and the forces of nature are completely impersonal. It's only in our minds that the cruelty of the elements seems to be directed against us.

Uncovered ears first feel the wind's bite. In very cold weather our blood circulation is altered; flow is increased to the vital organs of the body and reduced to the extremities, causing our ears, fingers and toes to tingle. If we are doing anything strenuous enough to cause heavy breathing, the cold air burns our noses and rasps our throats. Prolonged exposure to the cold without adequate clothing starts shivers up and down our backs.

Surprisingly, there are times even on the coldest days when the beauty of winter compensates for its misery. There were a number of these scenes last week. A pair of ruffed grouse, their feathers fluffed out to protect them from the cold, were outlined against the silvery morning sky as they picked buds in the top branches of an aspen grove. One cloudless afternoon, when the sky looked like a clear blue glass bowl over the white plane of earth, flocks of snowbirds wheeled away from the highway with their white wings flashing sunlight. There were orange-red clouds set in aquamarine at the onset of a winter sunset, followed by snug evenings in front of the fireplace with the wind howling around the eaves of the house.

There is another, less tangible, compensation too. There is a special reward for those who have endured the long months of cold, those who have felt the bite of the wind while shoveling snow, those who have known the patient waiting and have kept their hopes alive. Only they can fully appreciate the miracle of spring.

Winter Dawn

Let's begin today's hike before daybreak so we can watch a winter sunrise. Our long winter nights do have some advantages; it's possible to get a good night's sleep and still be up to witness the dawn.

Most of our early winter dawns were cloudy and filled with snowflakes. Those mornings have a kind of beauty, but the clear bright sunrises of recent weeks have been really fine. Usually I have trouble keeping my eyes open while I stumble to the kitchen for my morning cup of coffee; however occasionally I look out an east window first and the beauty of the morning banishes even the thought of food.

The eastern sky begins glowing nearly an hour before the sun comes over the horizon. Dark pines on the far shore of our little lake are silhouetted against a sky that is a lighter shade of gray. As the light increases, the background takes on a greenish hue. Then just before the sun appears, a rosy light tints everything in view. Finally the sun comes over the trees, flooding the whole world with radiance.

Most of our clear mornings have been frosty. The new sunrise reveals every tree and bush coated with a crystalline glaze, reflecting points of light like a forest of diamonds. The birch are particularly spectacular with their graceful trunks branching out to white frosted crowns.

During most of the year we see many more sunsets than sunrises. I am witness to late spring sunrises when I get up early for fishing trips. Deer hunting in the fall gets me up for a few more. One of my New Year's resolutions is to try to see the sun rise more often and to take time to absorb a little of the dawn beauty.

A recent trip renewed many memories. Those who join us regularly for these verbal journeys will recall frequent references to my childhood on a farm near Howard Lake, Minnesota, about 50 miles west of Minneapolis. There is some good farmland in that area, and ours was a pretty decent farm in the old days of horse-drawn farm equipment. Our land was hilly, the fields small, and the Crow River ran right through the middle.

After the death of my parents we sold the farm to the county to use as a park, which was named after my father.

At the corner of the old farm were a country store and a creamery, owned and operated by Uncle Charlie. The store sold groceries, work clothes, candy, tobacco, and a great many other items. It was a buying station for locally produced eggs. Perhaps most important Highland Store was a social center. The local farmers came in for a box of snuff, a can of beans, or a bottle of beer and stayed to discuss the weather, the crops or the latest local gossip. On cold winter days the coal-burning stove in the middle of the store kept the chill away for many an afternoon of Whist or 500. The dice box settled the question as to who would buy the next round of beer.

We went back to the store for a visit the other day. It wasn't quite the same. The old metal-sided building has been replaced by a new concrete block structure. The coal stove is gone from the middle of the room and the old wooden floor has been replaced by gleaming tile. I looked around and couldn't find a single spittoon, even though Copenhagen snuff is still a pretty good seller.

Highland Store is still something of a social center. Local farmers come in for a box of snuff or a glass of beer and stay to visit with their neighbors. Many of them are the sons of the farmers who shook dice and played Whist in the good old days.

Last weekend was another of those too-cold-to-go-outside periods. We did get to see a bit of wildlife from our living room, making me wonder if wild animals and birds know in advance when weather conditions are going to change.

On Friday morning, just at the beginning of our second bitter cold weekend, three ruffed grouse were feeding right in front of our house. They were picking ironwood buds and seemed to know just how far out they could go on the limber branches. Pecking buds one right after another and then flying to another branch to continue feeding, they were in a hurry. We knew that colder weather was moving in and somehow the birds knew it too. We were home all weekend and never saw the grouse family again. I suspect that they filled up with food and then dived into a snow bank to wait for warmer weather.

The small birds—chickadees, redpolls and juncos, were active too, continuing active feeding all through the daylight hours of the cold snap. I think they are too small to eat enough to last more than overnight. In spite of their insulating feathers they use up a great deal of energy, needing food every day to replenish it.

There are some indications that wild creatures can anticipate weather changes, although I don't put much faith in groundhogs seeing their shadows. I'm sure that no groundhog in its right mind would come out of hibernation on February 2 in this part of the country!

Major changes in weather are usually preceded by changes in barometric pressure. There is solid evidence that the feeding of fish is affected by changes in air pressure. There may be other signs that animals can recognize, either by instinct or from experience. Cloud patterns and changes in humidity are reliable indicators of changing weather patterns.

People used to be better at predicting weather before we had radio and TV forecasters. Doris remarked last weekend that the sunset looked cold. I agreed with her, but I couldn't tell why I thought it looked cold. I did notice that there were sun dogs almost all weekend, an old-timer's sign that colder weather was ahead.

Coyote Call

The other evening I heard the coyotes singing. That isn't an unusual experience in this part of the country, but it always makes me stop whatever I'm doing just to listen to their wild song.

We were late getting home from town, arriving at Fairview Farm just before sunset. We had been gone about eight hours and the wood fire was almost out. The dry wood in the basement was nearly used up, so I changed clothes and hurried out to chuck in some more wood before it became too dark for outside work. I was just finishing when I heard the coyotes calling off in the Pillsbury State forest to the north. The song didn't last very long, but I think they were singing for delight at the beautiful evening. A sliver moon hung high in the west with one bright star below it. The whole western horizon glowed crimson, and the coyote call seemed like a greeting to the coming night.

We used to hear the call of coyotes on camping and hunting trips, so I associate them with the western plains and the Rocky Mountains. They do seem to sing more out there, or perhaps the sound just carries farther across the plains. I have known for some time that there were coyotes in the Pillsbury Forest. Several years ago Walt Stark and I were snowmobiling in that area. Walt is the District Forester in Pillager and was helping me search for a snowmobile trail route west of Rock Lake. We came across a place where coyotes had caught a deer. All that remained of the victim was part of the skull and a few patches of hide.

The following autumn we hunted deer in that area and had to go back by jeep to haul out a buck we had shot. By the time we drove back in over the rough trail, darkness had fallen. Just as we were getting ready to leave the woods, we heard the coyotes calling nearby. It sounded like they were complaining about our stealing their banquet supper.

One disadvantage of a well-insulated house is that we can't hear the coyotes' song unless we happen to be outside at the right time. Coyotes do sing on summer nights too, but their song seems to have a different quality in winter, filled with cold and a hint of hunger, and the harsh facts of survival in the wilderness.

Farley, our golden retriever, has impressed us with his intelligence ever since he was a pup. He has learned most of the obedience-training commands, executing them well. Sometimes though I regret having taught him to pick wild berries.

We obtained the dog from a retriever breeder who lived about 80 miles from our home. My wife Doris suggested that we name him Farley because we had to drive so "far" to get him. When the pup was about six months old, we enrolled him in a dog obedience course, and Doris took him to the weekly training sessions. With rewards of cat food nuggets he learned "sit, stay, come" and "heel," and how to behave on leash. These sessions were held at the old Brainerd Armory. I remember that we had to carry the dog up the front steps on our first few visits. He could climb carpeted stairs at home, but couldn't manage those hard finished steps at the Armory.

At home I worked with the dog on retrieving, for which he seemed to have a natural aptitude. A year later we went to a guide /dog training course at a game farm which introduced Farley to the scent of game birds. He has developed into a fairly good hunting dog, though I can't seem to break him of chasing rabbits.

Farley is my almost constant companion. He goes out with me as I work on our Christmas tree plantation, and makes occasional contributions to the crop's well being by catching gophers and mice. He seems to feel deprived on the rare occasions when I drive off in the pickup truck without him.

The berry-picking business started a couple years ago when I was picking wild raspberries. I offered the dog a small handful of the sweet red fruits, which he ate with relish, looking for more. I decided that picking berries for the dog was too tedious so I showed him some ripe berries that he could bite from the canes himself. In a few minutes the dog was picking berries faster than I was! Later that fall Farley adapted his raspberry skills to wild blackberries and harvested the lion's share of these fruits that grew along our driveway. The following spring the dog discovered the delights of wild strawberries and blueberries. He had periodic snacks of fresh fruit all through the growing season.

In the winter months my most frequent hikes are out our driveway and back. The drive is about a half mile long, and a walk out to our mailbox and back is a pretty good daily exercise. Farley never fails to join in these winter jaunts. One day as we hiked the driveway, I noticed some bright red rose hips. I showed them to Farley and he picked and ate them just as he had the summer berries. Now the dog investigates the roadside bushes and picks a few frozen fruits on nearly every outing. He does such a thorough job of devouring the hips that I'm afraid there will be no seeds left to provide future wild rose bushes!

Get out your snow boots, a warm jacket, and your ear lap cap. Have all your cold weather gear ready, so that we can get out to enjoy the beauty of a frost-covered magic morning. You can never be sure when the magic is going to happen, so be prepared!

We had one of those times last Sunday morning. Dawn broke over a white world. Fresh snow covered the ground and every tree branch and bush was sparkling. There was a fog of ice crystals in the air too—even the air looked frosty. The far hills were shrouded as though we were looking at them through a lace curtain. The weather was cold, but there was no wind to damage the beauty of the countryside.

As we drove out to church, each of the small pines in our tree plantation was flocked with white. I've never really liked flocked Christmas trees, but somehow they look better when God does the flocking. Out on the highway we drove by a grove of larger pines, marveling at their frosted beauty. A bit farther on we noticed a stand of mature hardwoods, just as beautiful as the pines. We decided that our favorites were the birch trees; the delicate tracery, like white-on-white embroidery, had a fragility that made it unique.

I don't totally understand frost. Like dew it forms when the temperature drops below the dew point. This part makes sense, but the elaborate patterns formed by frost crystals are beyond my comprehension. At our house we try to regulate the humidity of the indoor air so that we don't get too much frost on our windows. Recently, however, we visited our friends, Don and Betty Turnquist, on a very cold day. Their house has large patio doors in the living room where the frost had formed elaborate designs. One of the doors looked like a painting of tall pine trees. Parallel tree trunks rose from the bottom of the glass and spread into leafy, branched patterns near the top. Don was going to try to get a photo of the frost. That would be a difficult assignment—I hope he was successful.

Red Rover and I went for a short afternoon hike following that frosty morning drive. There was still some beauty in the landscape, but the frost's magic had disappeared, although I knew that such a magic morning would come again. I looked forward to future frosty mornings, fairly common in early spring.

Winter Picnic

Picnics are usually reserved for warmer weather, but there is no reason why we shouldn't have them in winter too. Our whole family went on one the other evening—a very pleasant affair. There is a spot on the bank across the lake from our house where a small grove of sixty to eighty year old Norway pines stand, the prettiest trees on the farm and a perfect place for our picnic.

The weather was quite warm, almost a January thaw, which made the picnic even more enjoyable, although I have had picnics when the temperature was near zero and still enjoyed them.

Since we were hiking and the snow was deep enough to make walking difficult, we tried to keep the preparations as simple as possible. No picnic baskets or tablecloths; only the essentials. The menu consisted of hot dogs and buns, raw carrots and celery, coffee and milk, and marshmallows for dessert. We packed the food in a large plastic bag, taking extra plastic bags along to provide a dry place to sit. Add an ax to the mix and that's all we needed.

We picked an open spot near the towering pines, but found no convenient logs to serve as seats. There was a standing dead tree nearby and a few strokes with the ax made seating for the whole family. While Carla was down by the swamp cutting green sticks to serve as skewers, Chris and Kathy gathered birch bark to start the fire. Birch lights easily and burns with a fast hot flame, almost like kerosene. If only the loose outer bark is taken, its removal does not harm the tree. Tiny dead twigs from the lower branches of the pines, called witch wood, provided kindling, and branches from a dead oak provided adequate fuel.

The whole family enjoyed the fire until it burned down to make good cooking coals. In the midst of the woods, just after sunset, our simple meal tasted delicious. We toasted marshmallows long after our hunger was satisfied just because it was so pleasant.

As the woods darkened, silence settled over us, the only sounds the crackling fire and the breeze sighing in the pine tops. It was the perfect way to finish a winter day. As we carefully worked our way through the dark woods and crossed the lake for home, we were filled with contentment, much like we have felt after a pleasant outing on a summer evening.

The weather on the last day of January was so mild that we had to do something out-doors. Doris and I decided on a winter wiener roast for our Sunday supper. The thermome-ter showed a temperature of 48 degrees, the sun was shining, and the wind light and vari-able with only occasionally stronger gusts. The snow in the woods was nearly two feet deep, requiring snowshoes for a trek down to the south forty. We hadn't used the snow-shoes much because of the lack of snow during the past couple of winters.

I headed out a few feet ahead breaking the trail while Doris carried the backpack of food and drink. The trail-breaking was hard work. The snow was melting but had not yet become compacted. My snowshoe webs sank about ten inches, picking up a load of heavy wet snow with every step. Farley, our retriever, wasn't content to follow us, but went bounding ahead. He soon tired of jumping through the deep wet snow, returning to follow in our tracks.

We found a fallen tree trunk at the edge of the woods that offered a sheltered spot to sit in. I tramped the snow down, we took off the snow shoes, using one to dig a pit in which to build our cooking fire. I had detoured off the trail occasionally to pick up some loose banners of birch bark, as good as kerosene for starting a fire. I added dry pine twigs and then oak to make coals for cooking. While we waited for the fire to burn down, I cut sticks for roasting wieners, and then rested on the log with a soft drink.

I like my hot dogs burned on the outside and hot and juicy inside. Good quality wieners cooked over a wood fire seem extra delicious in midwinter. We finished off the meal with "S'mores," which are made by placing a hot toasted marshmallow on a square of chocolate sandwiched between graham crackers. They're called S'mores because they taste so good, everyone wants some more!

Farley drooled through the whole meal until we gave him a hot dog bun and a marshmallow so he could enjoy the outing too.

After my second S'more I built up the fire and then sat back to enjoy the winter sun-set. The sun was sliding behind the tall pines in the west. Overhead the sky was a clear deep blue, the western sky turning bright orange. A jet vapor trail left a light orange strip across the sky. A bit later the colors began to fade, showing lemon-colored clouds with strips of baby blue between, shading to lavender through the tree tops. As darkness moved in, some high purple clouds still showed. The snow pack reflected the light of a half-moon while the evening air brought with it a chill to remind us that it was still winter. We mushed back to the warm house with pleasant memories that will comfort us for the rest of the season.

"I like January," my wife Doris said. "It's so quiet." Doris is an Iowa girl and not overly fond of cold weather. The remark surprised me, but when I stopped to think about it, I could see her point; January is a peaceful time of year.

There is a sort of lull after the feverish activity of the Christmas-New Year holidays. The decorations are taken down and stored away in the attic and the Christmas tree is gone from the living room. Family and friends have departed and for a few days, the silence seems lonesome. A week later the quiet becomes a friend, bringing time for relaxing.

This year the weekend after New Year's also brought bitter cold. We had good friends out for a pheasant dinner on Friday evening, visiting in front of the fireplace so the low temperatures couldn't touch us. The next day I had planned to saw wood. I went out in the morning to check the oil in our old tractor and soon decided to postpone the outdoor work. The temperature was well below zero, a sharp northwest wind blowing fiercely. A few hours later the wind-chill factor was thirty-nine degrees below zero. I did get a bit of outdoor exercise throwing in wood for the heater, shoveling the walk and going out for the mail. I got just cold enough so that I appreciated the chance to stay indoors the rest of the day.

Our Saturday wasn't idle, but it was a day without any pressures. There was time for sharing an extra cup of breakfast coffee, to enjoy some good music during lunch and while reading the morning mail, to drive down to the country store, and then stop for a few minutes at the sport shop to see if any good used shotguns had been taken in trade. There was time to read some of those outdoor magazines that have been piling up next to my easy chair all fall, time for a few minor repairs around the house, and time for looking at the thermometer and shaking our heads. Doris was right; it was nice to have a quiet time.

Midwinter is the quiet time in nature too. There are a few winter birds around, but our squirrels seem to go into temporary hibernation on these cold days. We have enough snow to provide a good insulating blanket and the earth lies waiting as though it were sleeping through until spring.

Reports indicate that fishing has been good this winter, but when the thermometer shows twenty below, only the most ardent sportsmen are out. The ranks of skiers and snowmobilers are noticeably thinned, and even the number of cars is reduced. Perhaps people, like plants and animals, need a time of hibernation or dormancy. It seems that a few days of quiet are refreshing—a needed recharging before the busy seasons to come.

We've just completed the busiest fall ever. A late summer remodeling project stretched on so that we have been behind schedule with preparations for winter. Hunting seasons were later to the point where they overlapped our Christmas tree harvest. Outside of hunting and a very pleasant Christmas holiday we have had no time for recreation. There just didn't seem to be any extra minutes for our usual wood-making effort. We were so low on wood that we weren't using our wood-burning heater. We had to kick a few left-over chunks out of the snow bank to get fuel for a New Year's Eve hearth fire.

Finally on New Year's Day I had time to work on the wood. Our good friends, Dick and Joyce Kunz, were with us for the weekend. Dick is an ambitious fellow who seems to really enjoy physical labor. I thought it might be too cold, but our old jeep started with no problems, power for the wood hauling job. By supper on New Year's we had about four cords of oak and birch piled up next to the buzz saw. Dick wanted to work into the evening to get it all sawed up, but I knew that it was going to take some time just to start my old tractor to furnish belt power for the saw.

The tractor hadn't been started since mid-summer. I found the fuel valve frozen shut and plugged with ice. I had to remove the whole valve assembly and bring it into the house to thaw out. Then with fresh gasoline and battery jumpers the old machine sputtered to life. By the time I got everything lined up and ready to buck wood, it was three-thirty Sunday afternoon. I decided then to cut only a week's supply and postpone the rest until the following Saturday.

Soon after the sawing began our neighbor, Dick Reinhardt, and his daughter, Christie, walked over to watch. Dick had heard the ring of the buzz saw and knew at once what was going on. A big buzz saw has a distinctive ring that doesn't sound like anything else. I drafted Dick to throw the chunks as I cut them and we soon had a respectable pile of stove-length wood.

It was nice to have a neighbor stop by to help with the work. It reminded me of the old days when wood cutting was a community affair. In those days nearly everyone burned wood and neighbors would gather first at one home and then another until everyone had a winter's supply of ready fuel. It was hard, noisy work, but still enjoyable. There's a special feeling of security in having a large pile of good wood right outside the back door on cold winter days.

Usually we are much more interested in objects than we are in their shadows, however shadows are a very important factor in a winter landscape.

Our drive is bordered on the west by tall trees, which cast extremely long shadows, shading the fields for fifty yards or more. Long shadows can be seen at sunrise or sunset all year, but in winter they seem long even at midday.

Professional photographers pay attention to shadows. While color photos may turn out best on a slightly cloudy day, sunlight and shadow are the elements of good black and white photos. Our winter landscape is almost entirely composed of black, white, and varying shades of gray. I've tried to take pictures of snowdrifts with very little success. The graceful curves and ridges of wind-sculptured snow are almost invisible unless we have sunlight at the correct angle, so that the drifts cast dark shadows. It's difficult even to see a snowdrift at any distance unless we have bright light and contrasting shadow.

Shadows are important for hikers and hunters, even though we may not be conscious of them. The tracks we saw on last week's snowshoe outing would have been invisible without shadow. Compressed snow is the same color as the loose snow around it. It would take very sharp eyes indeed to notice the impressions left by animals if it weren't for shadows in the imprints.

Lack of sunshine can be the cause of some mental shadows that affect our outlook on winter. A series of cloudy days can make our winters seem endless. I like cloudy weather in the summer; it lessens the heat and reduces my chances of getting sunburned. In winter though I'll take all the sunshine I can get!

Clear winter nights seem to have a special radiance too, the air so clear that every star stands out in the sky. Moonlight provides interesting shadows with frost crystals sparkling like diamond dust just above the snowy landscape.

Contrasts between light and dark, winter and summer are what make life interesting in our north country.

I was looking through a gift book called, I Remember America, the other evening and got interested in a chapter on harvesting, then and now. It reminded me of a winter harvest that used to fascinate me when I was a small boy on a central Minnesota farm. In those days the local creamery was located at the crossroads, just at the end of our farm. My father was an energetic man, and one of his extra jobs was putting up ice for the creamery. We had no electricity then—mechanical refrigeration was unknown. Cream and freshly churned butter had to be kept cool on ice blocks.

When really cold weather set in each winter, my father checked periodically on the ice thickness in a lake near our home. When the thickness reached 24 inches, it was time to make ice. The first step was plowing the snow from a good-sized area of the ice's surface with horses hitched to a homemade snowplow. Then he scored the ice with a special implement called an ice plow, which looked something like a walking plow with a vertical steel blade about 3/8 inch thick. A team of horses with iron "corks" in their shoes pulled the ice plow across the surface, cutting a groove about a foot deep and two feet apart in parallel lines. Then the horses plowed another set of grooves at right angles across the first set, creating squares of ice partially cut through the ice surface.

Next came the hand-operated ice saw. This looked much like a crosscut saw about six feet long, but with handles only at one end. Father pulled it up and down to finish the cuts that the ice plow had begun. When he finished two parallel cuts with the saw, he used a breaker bar to crack the ice into 100 pound cube-shaped cakes. He slid the ice cakes out of the water on to the ice surface with ice tongs. A tripod with pulley and rope lifted the cakes on to a sled, which hauled them to the creamery ice house. We needed several hundred cakes to last through the summer.

At the ice house a special horse-powered elevator lifted the cakes so that they could be slid on to the growing stack of ice cakes, piled carefully in the center of the house with several feet of sawdust packed around the perimeter for insulation.

All through the hot summer the ice cakes were dug out as needed and slid down a ramp into the creamery's walk-in cooler. As a special bonus to my father, the creamery operator gave us a cake or two of ice each summer to use in making homemade ice cream, which was a very special treat in those days. Come to think of it, it still is!

Sundogs

The day of the sundogs began with a very cold morning. Our thermometer registered 25 degrees below zero and I wondered whether our pickup would start. I gave it a try at 7:30 AM, relieved when it sputtered to life. I decided to let the engine warm up a bit while I had one more cup of coffee before heading to work. As I started back to the house, I noticed a bright light in the east, like a short rainbow. Doris and I looked out the windows at a pair of sundogs, the brightest we've ever seen. They appeared to be about fifty yards apart and seventy yards away. They had all the rainbow colors: red on the inside, then orange, yellow, green and blue. I didn't know that sundogs ever appeared that close to the ground and wondered if it were some sort of optical illusion. We could see the trees across the lake through the prism of colors; it's a very small lake, so the distances couldn't be very far off. By the time I left for work, the sundogs were beginning to fade.

A few days later Clare Cahill said, "I had an interesting experience the other morning—I drove through a sundog." Clare lives on the Mississippi River northeast of Brainerd, about ten miles from our house. His description of color and distance apart sounded just like what we had observed. One of the sundogs he saw was right on the road. As Clare approached the spot in his car, he could see the sparkle of ice crystals in the air.

I looked up sundogs but about all I learned was that they are technically called Parhelia, common at the poles. I remember reading somewhere that they are caused by refraction of the sunlight by ice crystals in the same manner that rainbows are caused by raindrops.

The old-timers say that sundogs mean colder weather is coming. For that reason I've never been very fond of them. There aren't even any fables about finding a pot of gold at the sundog's end! Seeing them so brightly-colored and so close at hand was a thrill though. It was a sort of compensation for all the cold weather we've endured this winter.

Mead

My wine making hobby has just entered a new phase with the start of my first batch of mead. Most of my wines have been made from wild fruits, or at least from produce grown here in the north country. The primary ingredient in mead is honey, which I managed to get right here in Minnesota.

For years I have seen mead referred to in various historical novels, assuming it was an alcoholic beverage, but not sure what kind. After doing some reading on the topic I found that classic mead is a wine made by fermenting honey and water.

Mead has a long and interesting history. It was probably discovered by accident; honey and water mixed in the proper proportions will start fermenting from the wild yeasts that are always present in the air. Mead may have been the first form of wine ever made. There are references to it in the writings of the ancient Hindus as well as in those of the Greeks and Romans. Apparently honey was scarce in those days and they used mead only in religious ceremonies or presented it to royalty. The Vikings believed that mead had special qualities that promoted fertility. The drink was given to newly married couples during the first month after their wedding, giving rise to the still popular term, "honeymoon." There was a period in English history when hops and brewer's yeast were added, the result tasting like our modern beer. I'm planning to stick to the ancient recipe with a few modern wine making chemicals added to improve the odds of coming out with something drinkable.

As the art of beekeeping advanced, honey became the common sweetener throughout Europe and Asia and mead the common man's drink. Sugar from cane and later from beets largely replaced the expensive honey in the kitchen and on the table. For many years mead was made only by beekeepers. Nowhere is it a common drink today because honey for its making has become expensive, although there does seem to be a revival of interest among amateur wine makers anxious to find out how it tastes.

I have several recipes, some of them calling for rare honeys, such as orange blossom or wild rose. I am using mixed honey, mostly clover because most Minnesota honey comes from clover. Apparently mead can be made from any honey, but that made from milder-flavored honey is supposed to require less aging before becoming palatable.

The world of nature is often full of surprises. My wife Doris and I saw one just the other day, a phenomenon that neither of us had seen before—a winter rainbow in the northern sky. The sky had patches of blue between some heavy dark clouds. Doris saw it first and called my attention to a strip of color below the clouds, rather faint at first, but brightening as we watched. We could see the entire spectrum from red through violet before the light show ended.

This was not a parhelion or sun dog, which are fairly common in winter. Our winter rainbow was much longer than the usual sun dog and shone in the northern sky 180 degrees away from the sun.

Ever since the story of Noah and the ark a rainbow has been considered a beneficent sign, a signal that the worst has passed. Rainbows are almost always seen on summer evenings after a rainstorm has moved off to the east. On a couple of occasions I have seen a rainbow in the west. The rare rainbow in the west in the morning signals an approaching storm. I'm not sure what a rainbow in the north means; it may just indicate a rare combination of sun and clouds.

We studied rainbows back in high school physics labs. We shined a bright light on a glass prism and marveled at the seven bands of colored light that were projected on a white background. We were told that, in a rainbow, drops of rain act like a glass prism to separate the bands of light. Most of us have made our own rainbows with the lawn sprinkler or garden hose.

A few years ago one of our daughters gave me a glass pendant as a gift. My first reaction was negative; I didn't think a pendant was an appropriate gift for a man, but we hung it in a window where it would catch the sunlight. When conditions are right, it makes tiny rainbows that float around the room when the pendant moves. Now I think that rainbows are one of the nicest presents I have ever received.

Our friend Bill Carner called from Brainerd a couple of weeks ago to ask if we had noticed the snow fleas. The debut of the snow fleas is an early sign of spring, usually well in advance of the arrival of the first robin. Soon after that call the weather turned cold (not a good time to search for snow fleas). It wasn't until last weekend that I got out to look for these tiny creatures.

I soon located several fleas in the snow banks along the driveway. A good magnifying glass is essential equipment for a snow flea hunt. With a glass anyone can see them on the sunny side of a snowdrift at this time of year. These primitive insects are only a tenth of an inch long. With magnification it is possible to see their antennae and the spring tail mechanism with which they jump as much as six inches, size-for-size far superior to Superman's leaps over tall buildings! In fact it is hard to study snow fleas. Just when you get them in focus, they jump out of your magnifying glass' area of coverage.

On rare occasions the fleas may be numerous enough to make a snowdrift appear gray. Once my deer hunting partners and I walked a woodland trail early in the morning. When we came back on that trail several hours later, we found that our old boot tracks looked black. Snow fleas had come out by the millions in our footprints.

A snow flea does seem like an improbable insect and many people do not believe they are real. After church last Sunday I mentioned that I had seen snow fleas; several people laughed at the idea. Even one of my daughters says she isn't sure whether or not I'm joking when I bring up the subject.

I retrieved my old entomology textbook and found that snow fleas are listed under the insect order Collembola (Spring Tails and Snow Fleas). They are described as primitive, wingless insects, living on the surface of the soil in decaying vegetation. They are so small that they are seldom noticed, except in winter when they work their way up through the snow on mild, sunny days. One description I read says that the snow fleas are of the size and disposition of finely ground black pepper. They seldom cause any problem, though snow fleas sometimes are a nuisance around maple sap buckets, in mushroom beds, and in greenhouse soil.

The horned larks are back! We won't likely see them on any of our hikes through the woods because they prefer open areas and roadsides near weedy fields. Their return to our part of the country is often the first sign of spring.

It's really too early to hope for spring, but the return of the larks does mean that we are on the downhill side of winter. We first saw these birds on our way to church last Sunday morning. They may have been around for a week before we noticed them, often arriving during the first week of February. The ones we saw were along the road in a patch of grass that had been scraped bare by a snowplow. They prefer open ground where they can peck weed seeds or grain that has spilled from passing trucks.

Some ornithologists believe that the horned larks are the most numerous birds in the world, yet many people have never even noticed them. They almost always feed on the ground and take flight when anyone or anything approaches. They have some fairly conspicuous markings when observed with field glasses, but these are hard to identify when the birds are flying. Once a person gets to know them well, horned larks can easily be identified by their flight. They have an undulating pattern and almost invariably fly a loop, returning to the same spot they were in before being disturbed. They are slightly larger than English sparrows with brownish feathers above, light gray ones below, and a few black feathers in the tail. The head is conspicuously marked by a black bib and eye patches. The "horns", which give the bird its name, are small tufts of feathers on each side of its head, hard to see without binoculars.

Horned larks are widely distributed, nesting all the way from the central U.S. to the Arctic Ocean. Our bird book says that they are found in similar climates all around the world. In our part of the world they come back from the south in February, start nesting as early as March, and appear to be quite at home in the midst of a blizzard. A few weeds above the snow or a small patch of bare ground seem to provide adequate food for their survival.

I'm glad we have a bird that is hardy enough to come back in February. They are a welcome sign that spring is on the way, even though we may have two more months of winter before it arrives.

Spring

The Maybe Month

Only a few things can be predicted with any degree of certainty in March. This month can be a long, dreary continuation of winter or it can bring the sudden arrival of spring. Spring weather in March is rare in the north country, but it has happened. Our nice weather in February gave us cause to hope for spring in March…maybe.

We can be sure weight restrictions will be posted on our secondary roads and grass and forest fires might plague us. One would expect the ground to be so wet that nothing would burn, however last year's grasses and weeds dried out rapidly and the fire danger might be high even before all of the snow is gone…maybe.

The ice should go out of our rivers and creeks, maybe even breaking up on our lakes…but probably not. We may have some high winds, we may have bare ground, we may even have blizzards; we could have all three this March…maybe.

Spring bird migrations are fairly predictable. We can count on seeing horned larks and flocks of juncos, we might see red-winged blackbirds, bluebirds and robins…maybe.

The deer have already left their winter areas, so we are sure to see some of these graceful animals around the countryside. Skunks should be coming out of hibernation too. Chipmunks could be waking up from their winter naps by the end of the month…maybe.

We can depend on seeing pussy willows in March. The red oaks wouldn't even consider budding out that early, but dogwood will grow redder, and willow twigs will grow brighter yellow. We could even see some little green aspen leaves…maybe.

We could have thunderstorms in March; they aren't really that unusual at this time of year. The old-timers say that the last killing frost will come six weeks after the first thunderstorm. If it thunders in mid-March, it should be safe to set out tomato plants in early May…maybe.

There is another tradition that says potatoes should be planted on Good Friday. I have a feeling that folk wisdom comes from farther south. Some years we still have heavy snow on Good Friday! Easter will fall on the first Sunday after the first full moon following the spring equinox. It might be potato-planting weather by then.

We can almost be sure that March will bring us a great variety of weather. Certainly!

Weatherhill

The snowstorm may not have been a true blizzard, but it was the closest thing to it that we've had this winter. I spent the whole day inside putting up paneling in the kitchen. I had a really good view of the weather from Weatherhill. That's the name we've chosen for our new home. Perhaps we shouldn't choose a name until we've finished every room, but our family is very fond of naming things. Even before we moved here, we named the land Fairview Farm, partly for the view and partly because it is in Fairview Township, Cass County. We thought of several names for the house, an earth-sheltered dwelling built into the side of a hill. It is also a future retirement home, a bit smaller than our former residence. At one point my wife suggested calling it Andersons' Over-the-Hill. Weatherhill seems to have a bit more class and it fits the location. We are protected here from the north winds but exposed to the warm south and southwest breezes. Since most of our weather patterns move in from the southwest, we can often see them coming before they get here. Looking out southward we have a fringe of trees on the slope below our home, then a low rolling area that used to be a pasture. Beyond that are low hills, and then a wide expanse of shallow water, known locally as the Rice Bed. South of the rice bed is a range of higher hills we call the Saddle. Beyond that, on a clear day, we can see the tops of two more ridges. The farthest ridge has a tower that is fifteen miles away, just visible to the naked eye.

On that snowy March day the far ridges were invisible in early morning. We didn't know they were obscured by rain until the drops started pattering down around us. As the rain changed to snow, the Saddle disappeared. Then the Rice Bed was gone and, during the height of the storm, we could hardly see the old pasture just below the hill. There was more snow the next day accompanied by a strong northwest wind. I wouldn't have known about the wind if I hadn't walked out to the mailbox and back. Trees and the earth embankment at the rear of our home gentled the fierce north wind. Perhaps we should call the place Weatherhill during the summer and Snughill during the winter.

North Country Therapy

I went for a solitary hike one evening last week. It wasn't just for exercise but for some north country therapy. I had just returned from a two-day training workshop. The sessions had been interesting, but the long hours without physical activity had left me tense and irritable. I arrived home just in time for supper while the rest of the family left for town almost immediately. After dinner a little walk was just what I needed.

Red Rover came bounding out to join me. I decided to check out my deer stand, which is a quarter-mile south of the house. Nearly all the snow had melted, yet puddles in every depression let me know that the frost was still in the ground. I stopped by the place where I had dressed out a deer last fall. All the remains had disappeared but Red Rover's energetic sniffing told me that some odors still remained.

My deer stand is at the base of a scraggly dead jack pine on top of a sharp little hill. I have an old bucket there for a seat in a spot partially screened by broken branches. It was a calm, clear evening, the setting sun giving me enough light to see the features of the landscape. Trees on the far ridges were silhouetted against a glow in the western sky. Everything was peaceful and I could feel my tensions draining away. Red Rover came over to be petted, then found a comfortable place to lie down in the dry grass.

A couple of times his head jerked around as though he had heard something that was inaudible to me. I anticipated seeing a deer come walking out of the woods.

At first the complete silence was broken only by the sound of a truck passing half a mile away. Then I heard the call of an owl; from the rhythm of the call, it was a barred owl. Our daughter Carla says that the barred owl's call sounds like, "Who-Who-Who cooks for you?" A few minutes later an answering call, slightly higher pitched, filtered through the wooded hills to the north.

High up in the southern sky, a pale half moon shone. I sat and listened to the owls exchange questions, while a few stars began to sparkle. As my dog and I turned back toward the lights of home, I felt relaxed, renewed, and contented.

Snowshoe Hiking

Last weekend was my first snowshoe outing of the winter. Snow had been so deep, so light and fluffy, that I considered it dangerous. If I should fall in such deep snow, I wouldn't be able to touch the ground and would have no way of pushing myself up. I rechecked the snow depth and found that settling and thawing had reduced the snow level to just over two feet. In addition a crust had developed, making it safe enough to venture out.

I picked up a long stick to help me keep my balance, heading toward one of our tree fields, passing my old tractor and other farm implements almost buried in the snow drifts. There was considerable variation in the snow crust's strength. In some places my snowshoes hardly made a mark; in other areas the crust broke and settled an inch or so as I passed. In a few spots the crust suddenly gave way, the web tips trapped under a two-inch layer of packed snow.

I mushed across the drifts to the lumber shed that the children helped me build last summer. I had worried a bit about the strength of the roof, but the snow was so deep, I couldn't get up close to check it. I could see that wind had blown most of the snow off the roof and the structure appeared to be in good shape.

A few days earlier I noticed a pile of feathers in the woods near our driveway. The snowshoes enabled me to get closer to this scene of tragedy and found that some animal had made a meal of a blue jay.

I took off the snowshoes, tried walking over the crust, breaking through with every step, the going very tough. I called Farley, our golden retriever, coaxing him on to the crusted snow. For a few steps he was able to walk on top, quite proud of this feat. Soon he broke through, having a hard time getting back on top. In conditions such as these we worry about coyotes and dogs chasing deer. The deer's small hooves break through the snow crust with every step, while the dogs and coyotes can run on top of the snow and wear down their prey. I think that we haven't quite reached this condition yet. If the canines have the same problems that Farley encountered, they would be slowed by frequently breaking through.

Frequently I find fresh deer tracks in our driveway and wonder if the deer use the snowplowed lane as an escape route. I see no deer tracks in our Christmas tree fields. It appears that the deer come out of the heavy woods on the other side of our drive, move up or down the drive, and then bound over the snow-plowed banks back into the woods. I also see tracks of snowshoe hares along the driveway. These big rabbits seem to move through the deep snow with no problem. Their pure white winter coats make them almost invisible against the snow.

On our hike today let's keep watch for the first bluebird of spring, or the first purple martin, or the first anything! April is the month of firsts.

The first robins arrived in our area a couple of weeks ago, but it wasn't until last weekend that we saw them in our front yard. When they came, they descended in a bunch, ten of them hopping around. They must have been checking out nesting areas. The flock didn't stay long, but one pair remained, proclaiming their territorial rights from the tree tops. A flock of slate-colored juncos arrived on the same morning as the robins. A few days later the ground-feeding juncos were joined by several striped sparrows, the kind that scratch in the dead leaves using both feet at the same time.

The first mallards arrived last week. I heard them proclaiming squatters' rights at the beaver pond dam below the hill. A few days later I spied the first pair of Canada geese winging north. The ungainly great blue herons arrived about the same time. April also brought my first noon lunch on the banks of an ice-free river, a pair of mergansers flashing by.   A friend reported having seen the first loon, even though not common here until the ice goes out on our larger lakes.

A real spring tonic for me was the sight of the first meadow lark on a road side fence post. Its bright yellow vest trimmed with a black v-neck and the sweet liquid notes of its call are the essence of spring.

April has other firsts besides migrating birds. We've already seen the first moths fluttering against the window. The first mosquito was in our bedroom, one of those obnoxious ones that whine around the room for half an hour before landing for a meal on exposed skin. We haven't seen the first wood tick yet, but I heard on Twin Cities radio that the first had been reported in the southern part of the state. We can hardly wait for that!

The first skunks came out of hibernation weeks ago. The first chipmunk showed up in the front yard a few days ago. The first pocket gophers are back on the job, digging tunnels in the Christmas tree plantation. I shall respond soon with the first strychnine tablets of the season!

Changes in the plant world are so subtle that it is hard to mark any first. There can be no doubt though that buds are swelling and grass is turning green. Any day now we will experience the first thunderstorm of the spring. When that happens our north country will burst into full bloom.

Spring Moonlight

Doris and I took a little walk last Saturday night, accompanied by Copper King, our golden retriever. There was nothing very special about this walk except for the brilliance of the moonlight and the feel of spring in the air. We live half a mile from our destination—the county road. Our mailbox used to be there, just about the right distance for a healthy stroll. Last fall our mailbox was moved to the end of our driveway and now we seldom walk to its old location.

Saturday had been very pleasant, the first good thaw we'd had. Water was dripping from the eaves all day, in open areas the snow settled several inches, and on sunny banks the snow fleas were out. The weather was cool for standing around but ideal for a brisk walk. The wind was not the raw, bone-chilling kind we usually get in winter, but a softer sort of spring breeze.

The moon had been full the night before, a "snow moon," but the predicted storm had not arrived. By the time we started out, the moon was high in the east, glittering on the crusted snow. The road was a ribbon of silver and gray where the shadows of tall pines cut the reflected moonlight into strips. As we walked south, several star constellations were clear above us. Orion, the warrior with his star-studded belt, was almost straight ahead, and to the west the tiny dipper-shaped formation of the Pleiades was flanked by the flattened "W" of Cassiopia. In the north the Big Dipper was clearly outlined by the moonlight, but the Little Dipper was hard to see. The night sky had lost the crisp brilliance of winter and put on the softer, velvety look of spring.

Our ears gave us another hint of the changing season. The snow had lost the characteristic squeak that marks each step in cold weather; instead it crunched underfoot. The softened snow, not quite slush, had refrozen after the sun descended. The predominant sound in the air, as it had been all winter, was the snarl of snowmobile engines, audible now and then from every point of the compass. In the occasional quiet intervals we could hear the wind in the trees. Oak leaves still produced the dry-bone rattle of winter, and the sighing of the pines always sounds the same, regardless of the season. As we continued our walk at an easy gait, all our senses were alert, searching for signs of spring change.

We really know that it's too early for spring to arrive, but sometimes the reassuring markers are there ahead of the reality. It was our sense of smell that really brought us significant news. Copper King noticed it first, but soon there could be no doubt about the message; blowing out of the woods came unmistakable evidence: the skunks had come out of hibernation!

The loons are back—a sure sign of spring! They arrived on Pillager Lake just after the middle of April before the lake was ice-free. We heard their quavering call in the night and saw them the next morning.

The call of the loon is the essence and mystery of our lake country. Loons have three different calls, ranging from a weird laugh to a high-pitched repetitive screech, calls like no other bird. The loon's call reminds me of camping/fishing trips into the wilds of Ontario where these birds seem right at home.

Loons appear to be playful birds. I have often seen them flying just over the lake's surface with wing tips flapping the water. At the end of such a run they slide into the waves and screech in apparent glee.

Loons need a long run on water before they can take off, however once airborne, they are fast fliers. I have read that these big birds cannot take off from land. A few years ago a young, earth-bound loon became trapped by our front door. It was heading south toward open water, but couldn't figure out that it had to go around our house. I managed to catch the bird in my landing net and carried it around the house where it resumed its cross-country scramble. I wished later that I had transported the loon to a lake to see it safely airborne.

Loons appear to be good parents. On our Canadian fishing trips we often troll past a small island where loons are nesting. The male swims quite close to the boat as though trying to drive us away. The female remains at water's edge, covering the nest and lying out flat as though dead. My fishing partner and I have seen this behavior in exactly the same spot for three successive years.

Loon nests usually have only one or two eggs. The newly hatched chicks are able to swim at an early age, but are often transported on the back of one of the parents. This action protects the young from predatory fish, such as northern pike and muskie. Loons often travel in family groups and several families may join together as fall migration approaches. Most Minnesota loons fly south to the Gulf of Mexico where they spend the winter, working their way back north as winter ice disappears.

Nostalgia has become popular, taking the form of memory boxes. They come in many sizes and shapes, most divided into little compartments for displaying baby's first shoes and grandpa's old pocket watch. I am also collecting things, which recall pleasant happenings of the past, although most of my memories are too large to fit into little boxes.

My den is still unfinished and serves as a temporary bedroom while we work on the rest of the house. There are some advantages to an unfinished room. Whenever I want to save something, I just pound another nail in a wall stud and hang it up! One recent addition is a small color photo of the Witch Tree, a Christmas gift from an old fishing buddy. The Witch Tree is a twisted old cedar growing (perhaps surviving would be a better term) on a rocky headland on Lake Superior's north shore near Grand Portage. Legend tells us that the tree was sacred to the Indians in that area. It served as a place where they presented offerings of tobacco to the lake spirit. Later it became a landmark for voyageurs on journeys up the lake to Grand Portage. I have visited the site and marveled at its obvious age and the tenacity with which it clings to the windswept rocks.

Below the tree photo is a letter holder with a wild goose feather stuck in one corner, a wing feather from the first goose I ever shot. In front of my desk hangs a very special collage etching made by my daughter Carla in a print class at the U of M showing a woodland scene with a Witch Tree and a goose feather sketched as an inset.

I also have a fondness for deer horns, especially those from deer that I have shot. I have a nice pair of antlers from a Montana whitetail that Carla mounted on a plaque. Somehow the mount broke when we moved our furniture. The antlers are still intact, but the mount will have to be repaired. Since we acquired our new land, I have been fortunate enough to bag two nice bucks here at Fairview Farm. Both of them had antlers broken early in the year and were not at all symmetrical. They are hardly fit for mounting, but their lack of symmetry does not interfere with their memory value.
I wouldn't trade them for any trophy rack!

Most of the things we treasure would have no value to anyone else, but having them around, in places where we can see them, adds an extra dimension to our lives.

Blue Sky

In spring the sky has a color and clarity that can be seen at no other season. My wife Doris commented about what a big sky we have. We may not compare with Montana's Big Sky Country, but our present home does offer us a much wider view than the woods-sheltered home of our past. I would describe it as a "deep" sky, a rich blue that goes on forever. Our old encyclopedia says that the blue color is caused by the diffusion of the sun's rays in the atmosphere. Blue light waves, being shorter, are more widely scattered, giving the whole sky a blue color.

I believe the deep blue spring sky is due to the air clarity. With the ground saturated by snow melt, there is very little dust in the atmosphere. Plants have not yet developed the pollen that will permeate the air later in the spring. Smoke from forest fires may obscure the sky later, but for now the air is crystal clear. In contrast summer skies are often dulled by high humidity, in autumn there is a golden sort of haze caused by dust, and winter skies may hold ice crystals, imparting a lighter hue. A spring sky looks as though it was brand new and had not yet had time to fade. If we are fortunate enough to go out on a day when there are fluffy white clouds, the contrast makes the sky look even bluer.

One of my most vivid childhood memories is lying in a haystack on a spring Sunday afternoon, eating popcorn while gazing at the sky. Lying back is the ideal posture for sky watching, although in spring this can present some problems. The ground is too wet and cold to lie on. Using a blanket or rug for such a frivolous purpose would cause unnecessary laundry problems, therefore, the haystack seems an ideal solution.

In those days I lived on a farm that supported a variety of livestock. We had eight dairy cows, which were fed outdoors during mild weather. To facilitate this feeding we built a large haystack just outside the barnyard fence. When feeding time came we didn't want to open the whole top of the stack to inclement weather, so we cut off sections with a hay knife. This left a platform of hay that was snow-free and dry, an ideal place to lie and watch the sky on a sunny April afternoon.

The tree farm where we live now doesn't have any haystacks; we have to be content with brief views of the sky. A stiff neck is the result of looking up for too long.

Spring is a wonderful experience, hiking with the snow gone from the woods and the insects not out yet. We enjoy things like open water instead of ice, the sound of bird songs and frog croakings instead of winter silence. We appreciate the tinges of green that begin to appear on the landscape.

We hadn't even thought seriously about spring flowers until our daughter Kathy came in with a tiny scilla blossom, the delicate little flower bluer than a sliver of spring sky.

This started us looking for more blooms, but it's really too early for most spring flowers. The search was disappointing until I ventured out with a good hand lens. I recommend this practice to everyone who wants to enjoy the full beauty of spring.

Right outside our back door I noticed some rather odd-looking brownish clusters on the twigs of a Chinese elm. Under the lens they were beautiful maroon-colored blossoms, resembling miniature peonies. Down at the slough the blueberry plants were not quite in bloom, but under magnification the tiny pink buds were more delicate that any rose. Upon close inspection the alder bush had a double beauty. Last year's fruits, looking like miniature pine cones, and the newly-formed catkins, appeared on the same tree. The catkins looked like long flexible caterpillars, really roots of tiny reddish sterile flowers.

Many of us pick pussy willows for decoration and when they begin to turn yellow, chuck them in the trash. Before you throw them out, take a close look. Under a good lens the yellow color will be revealed as flowers, like a field of daffodils.

Other trees, such as the maple and basswood, will be coming into bloom soon and some of the nicest flowers will go largely unnoticed because they are so small—or perhaps because we are so big. Next time try using a hand lens and get a bee's-eye view of these beauties of spring.

My daughter Carla and I spent the better part of an afternoon cutting fireplace wood with our recently acquired buzz saw. This is a job that we usually do in the autumn rather than in spring. It's fairly strenuous work; still we find it enjoyable. Even though summer will soon be here, we wanted to have some wood on hand for those cool evenings we often have. There was a stack of birch and oak felled over a year ago. Occasionally I cut a few sticks with my chain saw, so we never ran out of wood. A chain saw is a very efficient tool for felling and limbing trees, although it can't compare to a buzz saw for cutting logs into fireplace lengths.

For years I have wanted a good buzz saw, but never had a good power source with which to operate one. This spring we bought an old farm tractor and then were fortunate enough to get an excellent used buzz saw too. When we first brought the saw home, the blade was quite dull and had lost most of its set. After having worked it over, it did an excellent job.

The weather on our wood sawing afternoon was cold and windy with a few snowflakes in the air, rather like early November. The combination of weather and the old familiar ring of the saw blade awoke childhood memories on the farm in central Minnesota. We lived in a home that was heated exclusively with wood. Getting in an adequate supply of fuel was a major operation. We felled hardwood trees with a two-man crosscut saw and limbed the trees with an ax. Sometimes we saved a few of the best logs for lumber and fence posts. We split others with a maul into slabs that could be easily loaded. Along with the poles cut from limbs, we hauled these slabs in to the farmstead with a horse-drawn bobsled. This work was done during the winter and the wood was allowed to season throughout the summer. The next fall it was cut into lengths that would fit the cooking and heating stoves.

Wood sawing day was a big event. One of our neighbors had a buzz saw mounted on a trailer and powered by a large one-cylinder gasoline engine. The whole community used the machine. Neighbors helped each other with the labor, and wood cutting became something of a social event. With winter coming on, it was a good secure feeling for all of us to have a big stack of wood. There was still a lot of work ahead, splitting, ranking, and carrying wood to the house, but we knew we would be warm all winter.

I still have some of that good feeling after cutting wood today. We plan to use more wood in the future to help conserve fuel, but so far we have used it mainly for the enjoyment of an open fire.

Alice's Hike

Spring must surely be in the air! One day last week Alice, our cat, joined Red Rover and me for our evening hike. I'm not really sure whether animals can sense changes in the seasons, but this was the first time since fall that Alice had been out of the backyard.

Alice has been a part of our family for nearly seven years. She isn't an enthusiastic partner in all of our outdoor activities like our dog Red Rover, but for a cat, she isn't bad. We received Alice from Mrs. Win Borden who had rescued her from extermination. Alice was a skinny, neurotic kitten and I wasn't sure that getting a free cat was any great bargain. After her first batch of kittens we had her spayed and she has grown into a calm, friendly cat.

If cats have nine lives, Alice has used up several of hers. On one occasion she came home with a back toe nearly torn off. I finished the amputation with the duck shears and in a few weeks she had completely recovered. Another near miss caused the loss of her tail. The cat had climbed up on the front tire of our car one winter night to be close to the still warm engine. When I started the car and backed out of the parking place, there was a terrible yowl and a partially disabled cat. She recovered except for her tail which had no feeling or muscular control. This time we took her to a vet for the amputation. She seems to get along perfectly well without a tail. We have become so accustomed to a tail-less cat, that we think it strange when we see a cat with a tail!

Alice was fully grown and well established in the house when Red Rover arrived as a small pup. After a few antagonistic hisses the cat decided to tolerate the new arrival, and the two have had a friendly truce ever since. It helps that Red Rover is an outdoor dog while Alice is a house cat. She has the run of the place when we are at home, but is confined to the back porch at night and when we are gone. During the summer months she is outdoors most of the daylight hours.

In nice weather it is common for the cat to follow along when we go for an evening walk. Usually the dog bounds on ahead and the cat trails along behind. If Alice gets too far behind, she starts a pitiful meowing. Sometimes we feel sorry and wait for her. When she finally catches up, she makes a mad dash up the road and, for a while at least, is the leader of the procession. On last week's hike she trotted along for the whole outing, even negotiating some muddy spots without complaint. Perhaps, like us, she had cabin fever.

Most days are filled with little things that are hardly worth mentioning when considered individually, but they add up , making life interesting.

The other morning as Doris and I were eating breakfast, a large hawk sailed over the tree field. It's nice to see them back from the south. After Doris, a music teacher, had left for school, I took time for a second cup of coffee and was treated to a visit from a small flock of purple finches, the first I had seen this year. One of them was eating sunflower seeds from the feeder mount on our kitchen window, a distance of only three feet from my view. It would pick up a single seed, get it lengthwise in its beak and begin to chomp on it. In a second a part of the hull would fall out of each side of its beak, the seed slipping down its throat. Then the whole process would begin once more.

Down by the blacktop road the pocket gophers were at work. Like most tree farmers I have no use for pocket gophers, but it was interesting to see them digging. It meant that spring had arrived and the frost was gone from the ground. During the noon hour I heard a robin pip-pip-pipping; a refreshing sound after a long winter.

When I came home from work in the afternoon, two pair of mallards were squabbling over nesting rights in the little slough down by the lake. Doris told me later that she had seen the first great blue herons down by the water's edge.

Before supper I had time for a walk. The lake water was still mostly ice-covered, but there was a 30 foot strip of open water along the shore. In the shallows some mud minnows darted about; I had been afraid they might have died from lack of oxygen this past winter. A muskrat came swimming by, climbing up onto the ice. I imagined that it was glad to be able to swim once more without a ceiling of ice covering its world.

Farther down the shore the low water level uncovered a small sandbar, and a deer's hoof prints told me it had been inspecting the lake. From the lake's north end I took a trail back to the house. The afternoon clouds were breaking up, revealing a brilliant red sunset. "Red at night, a sailor's delight;"—it should be a fine day tomorrow, filled with interesting little things that add flavor to north country living.

Old Barns

I have been noticing many old barns no longer in use. Some are in good condition, others are beginning to suffer from neglect. Strictly speaking barns are not part of the world of nature, but they are closely related to it.

You can tell the approximate age of a barn by the shape of the roof. The oldest were built with gable roofs, long straight rafters that came to a peak on top. Almost as old are the gambrel roofs, built with shorter rafters and higher peaks, allowing more haymow space underneath. Many old barns had cupolas. These little houses on the peak were often used just for decoration though some were part of the barn's ventilation system. They often served as pigeon roosts as well. In the early 1900s hip roofs became common. These used curved rafters, providing even more hay storage space. In recent years the gable roof has come back into use on pole barns, but those are generally one-story structures with no haymow.

The old barn I know best is on the central Minnesota farm where I grew up. It was a gable roof barn, rather small by today's standards. It housed only ten cows and four workhorses. Built by my grandfather long before I was born, the roof shingles and exterior siding were milled lumber, the rest of the structure built of native materials. The overhead joists were made from long straight tamarack poles which remained sound even after the rest of the building had begun to decay. The haymow was small and I had been thankful for that. The storage area had only one small door, and we had to pitch hay in and move it around by hand. I was jealous of the neighbors who had rope slings and track lifts that could place half a wagonload in one lift.

Haymows had the advantage of providing very effective ceiling insulation. Add to that the body heat of the animals and the old barns were warm and cozy in cold weather. Modern pole barns give adequate protection for cattle to survive the winter, but they are pretty cold places for people to work in.

I hope these old style barns can be preserved. They add such interest and character to the rural landscape.

Here we go hiking into May, which is not quite as unpredictable as April. We can be fairly certain of some things the new month will bring.

May is an exciting time for bird watchers. Some of our most colorful feathered friends will be back. Any day now the Baltimore orioles will be looking for a free feast from an orange-half nailed to a tree. A rose-breasted grosbeak usually arrives shortly after the orioles. Bluebirds and ruby-throated hummingbirds return this time every year. We are pretty sure that the hummers are the same ones who have visited us before. They often hover in the empty spot where the feeders were hung last year.

In a good bird watching May we'll see at least one scarlet tanager and an indigo bunting as well. The buntings are more brightly colored than bluebirds, so blue that we can hardly believe the color even when we are looking at it.

A few not-so brightly colored birds will be welcomed too because of their song. The soft cooing of the mourning dove is one of the most relaxing sounds around. A whip-poorwill, repeating its name over and over, fills a warm evening with soothing sound. A brown thrasher's planting song is definitely a part of spring. Ruffed grouse are with us all year, but it is usually in May that we first hear their drumming.

Wild flowers also add to the essence of May. Little purple violets hide in the grass and show themselves only when we search diligently for them. A shady ditch bank or ravine will show patches of old-fashioned blossoms called bloodroot and Dutchman's breeches.

Some of our wild fruits blossom in May—wild strawberry blossoms, the fragile little bells of blueberry, and chokecherry blossoms with their sweet-spicy scent hang in little bunches along the road.

Our forestlands show signs of May too. Tiny leaves on the aspens look like a greenish mist on the distant hillsides set against the darker green of the pines. Oak and maple show little red leaves, giving a rose-colored tint to a distant view. Later in the month delicate new needles on the tamarack will duplicate the hue of lime sherbet in the swamp lands.

May is tree planting time on our Christmas tree plantation. Some years the tree-planting plow turns up numerous white grubs. Farley, our golden retriever, walks behind the machine and loves to eat the juicy morsels.

May is one of the wettest months here, the moisture particularly welcome after new tree seedlings are in place.

Spring has come to Hole-in-the-Drive Farm! It arrived just one month after the official start of spring when the ice went out of our little lake on the night of April 20.

The breakup had seemed very slow in coming. A few days earlier Copper King, our golden retriever, had been out romping on the ice. Even on the morning of the 20th there was only a ten-foot strip of open water along the shore. When I came home from work that evening, half of the lake was open and the remainder was covered with floating slush.

Our daughter Carla took the canoe out, paddling through the slush to open water. Copper King decided to follow, breaking his own trail through the ice. He tried to climb up on the ice that he had played on all winter and seemed surprised that it wouldn't support him.

During the night a strong wind descended and in the morning the whole lake was clear, waves rippling across its expanse. I wish I could say that the waves sparkled in the sun, but we never saw the sun that day, and about ten o'clock snow began to fall. It kept coming down almost continuously for the next twenty-four hours. Still spring was here in spite of the near blizzard. The birds knew it; ducks, both large and small, swooped in on the open water to take refuge from the storm; large white gulls raised a clamor as they sailed over the lake or paddled in the waves. We don't often have large gulls. Perhaps they were visiting because Gull Lake, their regular home, was still ice-bound. A pair of loons moved in to take up summer residence. We were especially glad to see them, for the loon, more than any other living thing, symbolizes summer here.

There had been earlier signs of spring. Pussy willows along the lake had been out for several weeks. Tree frogs and spring peepers had been singing in the sloughs and ponds, the robins had arrived, and our friendly little phoebe had been investigating her nesting place under the eaves. The blue jays, who had been around all winter, seemed more numerous and noisy. The crows had been enjoying a spring feast on fish that died from lack of oxygen during the frigid months. They seemed to resent sharing food with the gulls; I've seen a solitary crow chase away as many as a dozen of the bigger white birds.

There is always some sort of wildlife to watch even in winter, but the numbers and species increases greatly when the ice goes out.

Farms can be attractive at any time, but it seems that they are best in spring. Recently I was scheduled to attend a meeting in Cambridge.   I drove down in late afternoon and drove back the following morning. The freshness of the farm country landscape made the trip enjoyable. It seems to me that there is nothing greener anywhere than a spring hay meadow. The slanting rays of the morning sun seemed to make the meadows even greener than they would be at high noon. Here and there a field of fall-planted rye or winter wheat contrasted their strips of green with dark brown soil between the rows.

I'm old-fashioned enough to still enjoy the sight of newly turned soil. Many of our more progressive farmers are using minimum tillage practices now, leaving most of last year's crop residue on the surface of the soil. Such practices are a great help in conserving soil moisture and professionally I endorse them. It's only nostalgia that makes the fresh-turned furrow appealing to me.

I suspect it is nostalgia too that makes me express a preference for farm land in the spring. I grew up on a farm and learned to know it intimately. Summer on the farm was a season of hot, sweaty labor. There were always a few good times at the swimming hole, but that was before I became acquainted with the sparkling lakes and cool pine forests of the north country. Farms are attractive in autumn when harvest fulfills the hopes of spring and repays the investment of summer's labors. Still I would rather invest my time seeking the wild harvest with rod or gun. Winter is a more relaxed season and a farm home is cozy and comfortable when cold winds blow. The field lands offer no resistance to the wind—snow collects in huge drifts along ditches and hedgerows and the soil is driven by the winds, turning the snowdrifts from white to black. Now when spring comes to the farm, it is like a resurrection. The dormant fields burst into life, the meadows are lush and trees start showing little green buds. I do like living in the woods among the lakes, but at this time of year, it's great to spend some time in farm country.

In the north country wildlife sightings are so common that we expect them all the time. In our area the second week in May was an especially active time. My wife Doris and I were part of the cast for The Geritol Frolics Show at Brainerd Community College. Others in the cast reported seeing both white pelicans and wild swans. Both of these large species of birds migrate through our area every spring and fall.

One night in midweek we were driving home after the show when our headlights reflected off something in the ditch. Suspecting deer I slowed down and drove safely past three of them feeding there.

We often see deer nearby, but the following animal only shows up once a year. We spotted it on the shoulder about a mile from our home. We got a good look at a full-grown coyote. The animal was skinny, but otherwise healthy, and did not appear to be afraid of the car. I turned into a neighbor's driveway and went back to see if we could get another look. The animal had disappeared and instead a large deer was standing on the opposite shoulder. I wondered if he was the buck that has been leaving large tracks in my driveway this spring.

The most spectacular sighting occurred on the following Friday as I was on my way to the forest tree nursery at Badoura. About two miles south of the nursery I saw something moving on the far side of a large meadow. This creature was about the right color for a deer but the shape didn't look quite right. A car following closely behind me made it dangerous to stop, so I never got a really good look. Half an hour later as I was returning home, I was pleased to see that the creature was a sand hill crane. The huge bird had moved to the near side of the meadow and was only about 50 yards from me. When I stopped my truck, the crane began to walk away and took flight as I stepped out of the cab. It gave a loud rattling call several times as it disappeared over the treetops. I have seen cranes only three times in my life and have saved a soft brown feather shed by one of them. It is a fond memento on my desk that helps me remember past crane sightings.

We have talked about the call of the loon being the sound that is typical of our north country lakes. However there are a number of other bird calls that signal the change of season here. One morning last week I took a hike down some of the forest trails near our home. Half a mile back in the woods I came across a ruffed grouse picking grit in the trail. The bird didn't fly when it saw me, but walked into the side brush and disappeared. The grouse population is quite low around our place; we only occasionally hear the male grouse drumming. This sound always reminds me of a one-cylinder gas engine putting fast when it's started.

For the first time this year I heard the soft call of a mourning dove. Far from sadness I feel peace and serenity in the soft cooing of a dove.

Wild Canada geese honk overhead most every day. We used to see geese only during the spring and fall migrations to their nesting spots elsewhere. In recent years geese are settling in Minnesota to nest; we hear them all through the summer. Even though their call is more common now, it still brings us visions of remote areas in the far north and a sense of wanderlust engendered by their flight.

On a more domestic note the phoebes are back, checking out the nesting boards under the eaves of our garage. Their call sounds like they are repeating their given name. Robins are on hand too, their repetitive calling bringing contentment to a mild evening.

I drove by the heron rookery near the south end of Gull Lake. Perhaps I should call it a heronry, a place where flocks of great blue herons have built their stick nests in the tops of tall dead trees. These cumbersome birds are quiet while tending their nests, however when they call, the sound is anything but melodious! It is a guttural squawk that sounds as though the birds are in great distress.

Most of our spring sounds come from birds, with a notable exception: the concert provided by tree frogs. We have two species of tree frogs in our neck of the woods, each making distinctive sounds. The spring peepers make a repetitive one-note cheeping sound; the gray tree frogs make a noise like a thumbnail running over the teeth of a coarse comb. It is quite common for both kinds to call from the same pond on a spring day.

Our hikes these days are often impeded by attacks of spring fever. Somehow lying in a patch of new grass and gazing up at the budding leaves against a spring sky seems more attractive than tramping through the woods. A blue jay flying by with a twig for its nest, reminds us that our lethargy is peculiar to the human animal. All other beings in nature are at a peak of activity. The birds, in particular, are busy with their home building.

The other morning we watched an oriole struggling with a piece of twine. The material was obviously well suited to the construction of its hanging basket nest. This particular piece of yarn proved too large for it to carry away, so the bird finally gave up and went in search of more easily portable material.

A pair of barn swallows has just finished their mud and straw nest in our garage. I have always admired the architectural ability of swallows, but this year they are not really as efficient as I had thought. The finished nest is neat and appears firmly anchored to the wall, but unfortunately was built right over the trunk of our car. The amount of mud that ended up on the car instead of in the nest is amazing! Perhaps the dry weather this spring has made mud of the right consistency hard to come by.

The scarlet tanager and rose-breasted grosbeak have just arrived but have not yet started to build. The phoebe, that nests each year under our eaves, has been incubating for a couple of weeks, and down by the lake mallard ducklings have already hatched.

Nests in our area vary in size from the hummingbirds' tiny thimbles of plant down and spider webs to the giant piles of sticks put up by eagles and ospreys. The intricately woven hanging nests of the Baltimore oriole show hours of careful weaving, while the killdeer manages with only a few small stones raked into a circle. The cowbird gets out of construction entirely by laying its eggs in other birds' nests!

To human observers bird nests have become a symbol of peace and security, but in the real world of nature this is an illusion. Many of the eggs so carefully sheltered never hatch, and a high percentage of fledgling birds fall prey to natural enemies before they learn to fly. However each species manages by special construction, seclusion, or sheer persistence to produce enough young to insure the survival of the species.

The First of May was garden planting day at our place. Some friends had planted seed several weeks earlier, while others maintained that there was still danger of killing frosts. We are still holding off on sensitive plants, like tomatoes, but the rest of the crops are at least seeded. Late frosts in the spring and early ones in the fall are the bane of north country gardeners.

This year it may turn out that lack of moisture, rather than heat, will be the limiting factor. Everyone I know is predicting a dry summer. An extremely limited rainfall in April surely makes it look as though they are right. I am making plans to drive a shallow well near our garden to provide irrigation. We are also using mulch to conserve water and help in weed control. Last year, for the first time, we tried artificial mulch— black plastic sheeting. This seemed to work quite well for vine crops, but results were inconclusive on other vegetables. Our sweet corn was not as good as usual, but our rainfall was so erratic that we don't know how the plastic sheeting would work in a normal year. The early part of last growing season was so wet that we had poor seed germination. By midsummer the garden suffered. The plastic did help retain soil moisture, but even so, the yields were not good. This year we'll use plastic on part of the garden and straw on the rest to compare results.

Most of the gardening articles point out the economic advantages of raising a garden in these times of rising food prices. I suspect there is some truth to these generalizations, but I wonder if the writers have purchased any seed this year. Most seed prices have tripled during the past few years. Prices for fertilizer and insecticides have also increased drastically, and organic materials' prices have risen even more than the chemicals. We still have some manure available from the days when our daughter kept a horse, but our sandy soil also needs chemical plant food to give us good production.

I have somewhat mixed emotions about the value of a garden. A few things, like vine-ripened tomatoes and fresh peas, are far superior to the ones that are available in the grocery stores. Home grown carrots seem to have better flavor too, but many of the other vegetables can be raised more economically on large truck farms. Still we do get a special sort of satisfaction from raising our own.

Soon it will be time for the first rhubarb pie this year. No one can question the value of a home garden while eating fresh rhubarb pie!

Let's go for a boat ride and look for some milestones along the way. Two weeks ago was the opening of the pike and walleye season—a major event in the north country. In recent years we have been planting trees on opening day and I probably won't get out fishing before our Memorial Day trip to Canada.

I wonder why so many people go fishing on the opener. Usually the fishing isn't that great, but there still are four times as many boats out as there are on any other weekend during the season. Perhaps some fishermen don't get out again until the next opener; or perhaps it's a reaction to the restraint imposed on them by fishing season having been closed for three months. It seems to me that the opener is a sort of milestone in their lives and it is important to react to its passing. It's one of the things we do to demonstrate we are still alive and making some sort of progress in the enjoyment of life. We need a marker to know that activity and pleasure have not ceased.

Have you ever watched the moon move? I have seen an eclipse on a couple of occasions. I was never sure whether the moon was moving or the shadow of the earth was moving across the moon. One night a few weeks ago when the moon was nearly full and low in the southern sky, I could see it through the trees as I lay in bed. From my point of view the moon's face was intersected by the trunks of the trees in our front yard. As I watched, the edge of the moon disappeared behind a tree. A few minutes later it reappeared on the other side of the trunk. With these trees serving as markers I could actually see the moon moving—something I had never noticed before.

I think there may be a basic human need for markers in life, like those tree trunks that enabled me to see the moon's movement. Perhaps that is one of the reasons that we celebrate birthdays and special holidays. Even annual vacations may develop into milestones that are important to the whole family. For children the school year serves as something similar. Students can hardly wait for the last day of school. Likewise, although many won't admit it, that first day of school in the fall will be just as important.

We regulate our lives by the change of seasons, and we are impatient when the weather changes don't keep pace with the calendar. For the outdoors person the hunting and fishing seasons are probably more in mind than the spring, summer, fall and winter seasons. Therefore the fishing opener is a milestone that must be observed. I suspect that the fishing fever that has become so acute recently has very little to do with fish.

I sat for a while out on the front lawn listening to the sounds of nature as the dusk of evening changed to the dark of night. Some of the sounds were the same as those heard during the day, but as night came on they seemed to possess a different quality.

Somewhere close a mourning dove called. I couldn't see the bird, but its low whistle was so distinctive that it couldn't be mistaken. Then a loon hurtled by overhead, its eerie scream echoing over the lake. We had seen a couple of loons earlier in the spring, but this was the first time that I had heard the familiar call.

High in an oak tree a robin began an evening serenade. I don't know another sound that conveys well being so perfectly as the robin's song at sunset.

A pair of mallard ducks squabbled softly in the slough just before a rain shower moved in from the west. The rain wasn't too heavy, so I stayed out to listen to the patter of the drops on fallen oak leaves. As the shower passed, the tree frog chorus started up. I realized that I had been hearing frogs all evening, but their peeping was so constant that the sound faded into the background unless I consciously listened for it.

Three ducks came over from the north—a lone drake loudly pursued by a drake and hen. Apparently the lead bird had intruded on the pair's nesting site and was not at all welcome. As darkness increased, the sounds decreased, both in volume and in frequency, except for the frogs. A squirrel chattered softly in an oak by the driveway, and two small birds that I couldn't identify came chipping through the willows by the lake. Off in the woods a great horned owl asked its eternal questions and, as the light disappeared from the sky, I heard the whistling wings of ducks heading north—perhaps the disturbed pair returning to their nest after driving off the invader.

These were all ordinary sounds of a spring evening, but they seemed to have a soothing quality that is absent when heard at midday. Perhaps the difference in quality is in the mind of the hearer rather than in the sounds themselves. Except for the frogs, the loon, and the quarreling ducks, all of the evening sounds were relaxing, and even those raucous exceptions didn't disturb the peaceful scene.

Summer

June Is

Every month (with the possible exception of February) has its good points, but June is something special. June is really many things special. Let's talk about a few of them.

June is weather with variety. It can be warm sunshine and gentle breezes and fluffy white clouds chasing shadows across the valley. It can be violent thunderstorms raging across the land, or slow long-lasting drizzle that nourishes all living things. June is nights that are finally warm enough to allow sleeping with open windows. It is June bug beetles rattling their wings on the screens and a whippoorwill whistling us to sleep with a repetitive call.

June is the eerie laughter of a loon on a secluded lake, and the soft sad whistle of a mourning dove from its perch on the roadside electric wires. It is robins listening for worms in the dewy grass of morning and singing their joy from the evening treetops.

June is the season of vigorous growth. It is hardwood trees finally come to full leaf, making the whole countryside green, and casting welcome shade on a hot afternoon. It is the candles of new growth on pine trees stretching in the sunlight. It is farm crops covering the fields with promising green. It is gardens that need weeding again, and lawn mowers humming in the cool hours of morning or evening. June is rhubarb pie and fresh crisp radishes. It is clover blossoms in hay fields and wild strawberries in road ditches that taste as sweet as our childhood memory of them.

June is brides hoping for sunshine and farmers hoping for rain and kids that don't care what the weather is like as long as there isn't any school. June is family vacations and swimsuits and fishing rods. It is lying on the beach, sitting around a campfire, and sleeping in a tent with raindrops pattering on the canvas. It is sunburn and mosquito bites and wood ticks and poison ivy. It is family reunions, and horseshoe pitching contests, and softball games.

For me June is a month of contrasts. Part of it will be spent in hard physical labor shearing Christmas trees. The job has to be done during the last half of June and the first part of July. Some of the days will be nice for outdoor work, but we almost always have some of our hottest weather during this period. Some of my time will be spent on a cool Canadian lake exploring among the islands and fishing for walleyes and northern pike. A few in-between days will even be spent on my regular job, working on soil conservation programs for the state.

Fur, Feathers, and Fins

We spent the weekend on a camping-fishing trip to Ontario. It was a good outing, but my memories of it are more about animals and birds than fish.

My partners on the expedition were Dick Kunz, my old fishing buddy from Duluth, and my daughter Carla from Minneapolis. We went to Dashwa Lake near Atikoken and camped on an island where we have stayed many times. Mosquitoes and black flies were there to greet us, but we were pleased to find that no one else was camping on our island.

As soon as we landed we saw evidence of wildlife. There were fresh moose tracks in the wet sand where we beached. We later found other signs that showed that a moose had spent considerable time on the island. We were a little concerned that the big animal might resent our presence and come charging into camp, but we never did see that moose.

There is some sort of diurnal varmint that lives there. In past years it has broken into our supplies and eaten part of our bread and cereal. This year we took a metal box in which we could store everything except canned foods. Still the mystery animal came into our camp every day while we were fishing. It knocked over bottles and cans and chewed holes in our garbage sack. There was no serious damage, but our camp was always a mess when we returned!

Our animal sightings were only brief encounters. As we trolled along a steep shoreline, we saw a mink scramble across the rocks and into the woods. We moored the boat in a sandy bay one afternoon and watched a pair of otters come swimming down along the shore. On our way home in the truck a red fox trotted across the road carrying a rabbit in its jaws. A few miles farther along a timber wolf loped across the highway in front of us.

Birds were around us every day. One big white gull had a nest on a rocky reef near our fishing spot. Every time the boat came by it climbed up on top of the rock to keep an eye on us. We were impressed by the location chosen for a raven's nest, containing four nearly grown birds. It was built in the cleft of a high rocky cliff. There was a rock overhang above it and a sheer drop to the water below. That nest was protected from the weather and safe from predators. The birds were with us even at night. A ruffed grouse somewhere on the island drummed every morning and evening. During the still nights we could hear a barred owl calling from the far shore. Many times we awoke to the eerie calling of loons, although we didn't mind being disturbed. The call of the loon is the essence of north country lakes. We just smiled to ourselves and went peacefully back to sleep.

I am writing this verbal hike in what I call my den. It is a second story room with windows looking out to the east of our little lake. The scene from this window is quite relaxing.

The smooth lake surface reflects the woods on the far shore in perfect detail. If we had the scene in a photograph, it would be almost impossible to tell which should be the top or bottom of the picture. Not only the shapes but the colors of the trees are faithfully mirrored.

We have two kinds of aspen growing on the lake bank. One is a bright, slightly yellowish-green while the other is a light gray-green. The white birch trunks stand out among the new foliage. The new oak leaves have a pink tinge while the pines are a dark, more mature green.

Patches of blue sky show between white clouds tinted rose with sunset light. These too are reflected in the lake's surface. A crow flaps by on the water's far side, its black image showing between the mirrored treetops. Swallows flit about after insects, their reflections following every dive and turn.

There is no evidence of a breeze, but some breath of air must have disturbed the water. The slight movement gives the illusion that the leaves on the reflected trees are moving, while the real ones remain stationary. A muskrat comes paddling across the lake, his v-shaped wake distorting the reflections. In a few minutes the ripples of its passing are gone and the double picture is restored to perfection.

The evening sounds seem a fitting accompaniment to the water and woodlands. Tree frogs provide a constant background chorus to a kingfisher's rattling cry from one end of the lake and the cry of a loon from the other. Outside my window a catbird is doing its imitations of other birds' calls while throwing in a few notes of its own.

Night begins to settle over the scene, but still the reflections are clear. We like living near water because its appearance changes so often. On calm evenings like this the mirror effect of the lake doubles our pleasure.

The Old Boat

Let's walk to the end of the lake to see if the remains of the old boat are still there. Almost every small lake has the skeleton of an abandoned rowboat somewhere along the shore.

Boats have always had a special attraction to most males. Children are invariably attracted to water, and after getting wet a few times the idea always occurs to contrive some means of floating on the surface. What boy has not constructed a raft or attempted to use an old wash boiler for a boat? I can remember how my friends and I searched the banks and bars of the river every spring. Our fondest childhood hope was to find a boat, perhaps one that had been discarded or, better yet, had drifted away from its owners and been carried on the current to our part of the water. We never did find one, but the hope recurred every spring.

When my wife and I first moved to our present home, we had no boat, and when I first saw the old relic at the end of the lake that old nostalgic feeling returned— that feeling of hopeful expectancy. Perhaps we had really found a usable craft, or at least one that could be rebuilt. The first close examination showed that it was beyond repair, discarded and forgotten years ago.

It had been a thing of beauty in its day as so many of the cedar strip boats were. Built by a real craftsman, every rib was perfectly spaced, each strip bent, tapered, and fastened with brass screws to give a grace of form not found in many boats today. Surely it had served well for many years, moving silently through the lily pads searching out the elusive bass. Many misty autumn mornings had found it concealed in the rushes, waiting for the whistle of mallard wings in the early dawn. Time, neglect, and winter ice had put an end to its usefulness, but it still remains a memento of better times.

Trillium

Driving early last week I noticed trillium in bloom. I stopped at the Swedish Timber House on the west side of Gull Lake to get a look at the many wild flowers growing there. We are near the end of the blooming period for trillium, but blooming was somewhat delayed this year because of the cool spring weather.

Trillium is a conspicuous wild flower of the lily family. It grows in damp woodlands of the United States, Canada and Asia. The name trillium comes from the Latin word triple. It has one flower per stem, each flower having three petals, and each white blossom backed by three green leaves.

For many years in the spring we have traveled to Ontario for lake trout fishing. On each of these outings we have seen trillium along the roadside woodlands. I have admired these pretty white flowers every year, but discovered only recently that the petals turn pink, sometimes streaked with purple, as the blossoms mature. In some areas this flower is called wake-robin because it blooms when the robins begin migrating north.

World wide there are about twenty-five kinds of trillium, but only two are found in our part of the country. By far the most common is the large-flowered trillium, which grows from New England west to Minnesota. Less common is the nodding trillium with blossoms that droop below the leaves. Sonny Anderson reports seeing a few of these on the Swedish Timber House grounds. This species is more common in Manitoba, Quebec and Newfoundland.

Our old encyclopedia describes trillium as wild flowers, but adds that gardeners can grow them. It suggests raising them from seed or transplanting them from the wild. I had heard that it was against Minnesota law to pick or dig these flowers although I wasn't sure if that was fact or fiction. I called Ron Miles from the Department of Natural Resources who reported that trillium are indeed protected plants in Minnesota. I asked Ron about other protected wild flowers. I know that the pink lady slipper, our state flower, is protected. This plant is a wild orchid and all of our wild orchids are protected. When road building or other construction might destroy some of these protected plants, arrangement must be made to move them to a safer site.

Most of our native wild flowers have rather small, inconspicuous blossoms, but the large-flowered trillium lends a splash of color to our spring woodlands.

Early this spring a pair of barn swallows moved into our garage. They had a great deal of trouble getting their mud nest constructed. After hours of carrying mud and straw their net result would be an untidy mess decorating the car's trunk which had been parked under their construction site. This happened several times, but finally the nest was anchored around a nail in the wall.

When the eggs hatched, the adult swallows apparently declared war on our cat. Whether the birds knew instinctively that cats were dangerous, or if the cat actually molested the nest, we never did find out. At any rate the swallows were determined to keep the cat away from their offspring. The appearance of the feline in the yard brought on a particular high-pitched call from whichever swallow saw her first—and the attack was on! Repeating the same cry the swallows took turns diving at the cat until she left the area. This went on for several weeks while the young swallows matured. One day the attacks stopped, and we discovered that the youngsters had learned to fly.

And how they could fly! Perhaps learned to fly is the wrong term; they could hardly have learned so much in just a few hours. They followed their parents in graceful turns and dives so complex that they surely had inherited that ability and grace rather than learning it.

Young animals all seem to have instincts which help them to survive but they apparently do not inherit fear of humans. In our driveway the other day a covey of young grouse was crossing . We had to stop our car and wait for them to get out of the way; they seemed not at all alarmed, even when we sat and watched them for awhile.

Now and then we see examples that seem like real intelligence. Our neighbors feed the birds all year. They are frequently visited by a downy woodpecker with rather shabby plumage that they have named Herr Schnabel. This summer Herr Schnabel became a father, and demonstrated an intelligence beyond expectation. Instead of carrying food to his youngsters, who are apparently not yet able to forage for themselves, he brings them to the tree where the suet feeder is located and stuffs them full of food with very little effort on his part. Is this instinct? Perhaps the first time was accident and subsequent visits were repetition. Perhaps it is what we think of as intelligence.

Mixed Bag

Our nature observations recently yielded a mixed bag—two birds and a barking fox. The first incident was the sighting of a brood of baby killdeer right on the edge of town. I had noticed the adult birds for several weeks and assumed they might be nesting nearby. I've seen killdeer nests consisting of only a few pebbles raked together into a rough circle to keep the eggs from rolling away, but I've never before seen the young birds. Most young birds have a different plumage than the adults, but these youngsters were miniature copies of their parents, bearing the white breast and throat with twin black collars, except that instead of flying, they ran and hid in the grass. They did a good job of hiding too. When I returned a few minutes later with my camera, the adults were still on hand, but I could find no sign of the young. Incidentally the name killdeer has nothing to do with deer. It is a verbal imitation of the bird's two-syllable call.

On the following day we were driving along a back road near Gull Lake when we came upon an American woodcock at the road's edge. These long-billed birds are rather rare and usually seen only in thick brush or remote meadows. Except for spring mating they are rarely seen at all, unless one is hunting them with a trained dog. They are interesting because of their odd appearance, but too small to be considered real game birds.

Our daughter Chris was the one who first saw the red fox down by the shore of our little lake. We all rushed out for a good look. It stopped near the lake's edge and looked back toward us. It barked softly a few times and then gave the typical sharp, high-pitched yip that sounds like a cough. It moved slowly along the shore and every few steps it would stop, look toward us and bark sharply. This performance lasted for several minutes while we wondered what it was barking at. Perhaps the fox had caught sight of our golden retriever pup—he is almost the color of a young fox, and our visitor may have been calling to a distant relative.

This was a first for me. I have seen foxes and heard them barking in the distance, but never before have I actually seen one bark. It came back and barked for us again, but we didn't really appreciate it the second time—it was at 5 AM!

Sounds of the North

Four loons were playing on our lake one morning, their wild cries echoing across the water. Perhaps this sound is more than typical in our area. Perhaps it's part of the essence of the north.

It was misty and rainy but the loons seemed not at all inhibited by the weather. One of these huge birds uttered that high-pitched laughing cry and then started swimming as fast as it could using its wings as oars to push along. Another flew just above the lake's surface, wing tips slapping the water at every beat, making a noise like a motorboat. Then it folded its wings and slid across the water. Apparently proud of this display it raised almost out of the water and began a different kind of call. This cry had only two notes, repeated several times at a very high pitch. It reminded me of a bull's bellow, only about four octaves higher. Perhaps it was part of the mating ritual, but it seems late in the season for mating. The feeling I got was that the loon was just doing it for fun. Whatever the significance its call added to the wilderness feeling.

There are other sounds that are part of the magic of the north. Waves lapping against a rocky shore, not violently like ocean breakers, but with some of the same feeling of power and eternity. Aspen leaves rattling in the breeze produce a characteristic sound. Sometimes, especially in the fall, they sound like raindrops falling.
One of the constant sounds is the sighing of wind in the pines. It is sometimes a lonely sound and other times a sound of unhurried contentment.

In spring and again in autumn we hear the drumming of the ruffed grouse. When I first moved to the area, I thought that my neighbors had small gasoline engines which I could hear putting as they started up—that's what a drumming grouse sounds like. For those who really know the country there are a number of bird sounds that are common. The veery, one of our less conspicuous thrushes, has a whining trill followed by an echo that I have heard nowhere else.

All in all the loon was an excellent choice as the Minnesota state bird, partly because of its eerie cry, but if I had to choose my favorite sound to symbolize the north, I would pick one that is with us all year long—the soft voice of pine trees whispering in the wind.

Thunderstorms

Thunderstorms develop most often on those hot, sticky days when it is an effort to breathe. The sky has a hazy appearance, but the haze isn't heavy enough to be called a cloud. The sun blazes down, with nothing to soften its fierce blast, and the light south breeze is so hot that it has no cooling effect.

Late in the day the thunderheads begin to boil up in the west. We hope that they continue to grow, at least enough to cover the sun and give some relief from the heat. An occasional spear of lightning flashes from one cloud to another as they build. The sun is covered and the horizon looks dark and menacing except in the east where the highest clouds still catch the sunlight.

What little breeze there might have been drops off and the whole atmosphere is oppressive. The thunder grows to a steady rumble, almost like the sound of jet planes passing overhead, and then the rain begins. Out in the open one can often see it coming, like a filmy curtain drawn across the land. The first drops are large and scattered, bouncing off the oak leaves or raising tiny geysers on the lake's surface. A few small hail stones bounce on the lawn, followed by the rain coming down in torrents. Wind is also part of the pattern and all the trees bow before its force.

Usually the storm doesn't last long, but passes on to the east, leaving the land cooled and refreshed in its wake. Both field and forest are a darker, cleaner green, and the setting sun glistens from jewels of moisture on leaf and blade. A rainbow appears in the east and robins chirp their evening song with renewed vigor, as though refreshed by the moisture.

As the storm moves on, the wind shifts, now coming from the north or northwest. The temperature and humidity drop, the western sky begins to clear, and the clouds in the east pick up the reds and pinks of the setting sun. Even the mosquitoes aren't quite so bad in the cool breeze, and we can enjoy an evening stroll. Life is worth living again!

After a Hard Day's Work

Most of our time recently has been spent shearing Christmas trees. The job is finally done for another year and it's a good feeling to have it completed.

For those not familiar with the process, our Norway pine trees have to be shaped by shearing to produce the quality that today's market demands by cutting off part of the new growth each year, producing a dense symmetrical tree. We do the job with long-bladed knives similar to a chef's roast slicer. The new growth is fairly tender and the sharp knife will cut it with a minimum of effort. Motorized trimmers are available, but most tree growers prefer to use knives.

There is a limited time each year when shearing can be done to produce the desired results. Running from mid-June through early July our present operation requires about forty days to complete.

There are some rewards for nature lovers during shearing season. Each day we find sparrows' nests within the trees, some with little blue eggs and some with hatchlings. This year we found a mourning dove's nest, and once during lunch break, a deer came out to watch us eat.

Weather can play an important part too. This year the early part of the season was pleasantly cool, frequently interrupted by rain. The last few days were sunny and hot, tempered by a breeze. Each day we start work while dew is on the grass. Wet feet are a minor inconvenience compared to the heat that will come later. By mid-afternoon our energy begins to decline. The younger members of the crew start talking about how nice it would be to go swimming while I am thinking about the cool air in our earth-sheltered home.

A shower, clean clothes and a good supper revive the spirit, and the cool evenings are pure delight. The sun that seemed so merciless during the afternoon now casts long cool shadows. The wind that was a lifesaver out in the fields is now brisk and makes us think about throwing on a jacket for our late evening stroll. The soft whistle of a mourning dove adds peace to the evening after the shearing job is done.

Fog

July brings a variety of weather. Some days are oppressively hot and humid; some are bright and cool, near perfection; some have morning fog. Fog can completely change the appearance of the landscape and create different moods in those who observe it.

Early one foggy morning I took a little time to enjoy the new day. We had opened windows the night before and the whole house was cool and comfortable. Outside, the world seemed to be hidden by a white curtain. I could see only as far as the trees that are twenty yards from the house.

Fog gives me a special feeling of solitude. Our house is located in a spot that gives us almost complete privacy, but when the fog settles in, it's as though the rest of the world disappears, leaving just the house and a few nearby trees. As I watched out the window, a small bird appeared in the white space between two trees. It was as though it had flown in from another world or had magically appeared within the white fog curtain.

Fog is a fragile thing, especially on a summer morning. A light breeze was causing the aspen leaves to tremble while the white curtain was becoming translucent. There was a pale glow in the east where the sun was trying to break through. I could see the tops of trees on the other side of the old pasture floating on beds of fog. A bit later I began to hear the rumble of thunder. A storm was moving our way.   Soon the thunder became a constant rumble and steady rain began to fall. The morning fog was washed away, but now rain obscured the distant hills. By noon the clouds were breaking up, the sun came out, the temperature began to rise, and soon my cool foggy morning had turned into a sweltering hot afternoon. We retreated to the lower level of our earth-sheltered home where the temperature remains constantly temperate and spent most of the afternoon visiting with good friends. The day ended with fog again. This time it collected in the low areas like a silvery moonlit blanket.

Wind and Light

Let's spend a few minutes watching the patterns of wind and light on the water. Heat, high humidity, and hordes of mosquitoes have taken some of the joy out of hiking in the woods, but those of us who live here can often enjoy some of nature's beauty right at our own front door.

As I write these words, a brisk wind is blowing across the little lake in front of our house. The morning sun, dimmed by a light layer of clouds, is still bright enough to make golden highlights on the ripples in the water. The wind is from the southeast and I can see wind streaks running across the lake. Wind streaks are hard to see from ground level, but from the windows of my second floor den, they are fairly obvious. Aviators, especially those who fly float planes, are always aware of wind streaks, which are a great aid in landing a seaplane.

In addition to the pattern caused by the prevailing wind, gusts create interesting variations. Gusts will cross the main pattern or they may be fast moving swirls moving in the same general direction. Each type prints a brief pattern on the lake's surface and then disappears. I have seen similar patterns in tall grass meadows and in grain fields, but they are easier to see on water.

Residents in this area always seem to be attracted to water. I'm sure one of the reasons is the great variety of visual sensations offered by the water's surface. Lakes are almost the only shadow-free areas here in forest country. Most of us like the forest, but it's nice to find an opening where we can get a broader view of our world.

After sunset the glow in the west is often reflected for a considerable time after the sun has disappeared from view. Even on a dark night there seems to be some light over the water. A whole new atmosphere is created by moonlight. One of the major factors that made us fall in love with our present home is the sight of the rising moon reflected in ripples on the lake on a breezy summer night.

On calm days the water's surface reflects a double view of the beauty around us. Our north country has something of beauty almost anywhere and any time we look, but our lakes increase the variety of visual impressions.

Wildflowers or Weeds?

The whole countryside seems in bloom, but sometimes it's hard to tell if we are looking at flowers or weeds. The state of Minnesota has a weed control law that lists a number of noxious weeds that must be controlled; it is illegal to sell crop seed that contains any noxious weed seeds. Most agriculturalists say that a weed is any plant that is growing out of place. For example corn is one of our most valuable farm crops, but if volunteer corn plants are growing in a soybean field, they are considered to be weeds. Identifying weeds becomes a question of location rather than species.

We once spent a weekend in Minnesota's Arrowhead. While there we drove a great many back roads and marveled at the beautiful roadside flowers. One that we found particularly attractive was orange hawkweed. My wife Doris wondered if we might be able to transplant some of it to our yard. I know that hawkweed, classified as noxious, should not be moved to an area where it could spread to adjoining farms. However, along the forest roads hawkweed is a beautiful wildflower and seems to do no harm. The reddish-orange flowers were a nice contrast with the white daisies and purple lupine.

Sometimes the decision labeling a plant a weed depends on local custom. In the suburb dandelions are persistent pests in well-kept lawns. On the other hand it is possible to buy improved strains of dandelion seed to plant in gardens for use as greens. Quack grass is listed as one of Minnesota's noxious weeds, but some of the commercial seed-cleaning businesses save up quack grass seed and ship it overseas for use in erosion control plantings on roadsides and ditch banks.

We have had some interesting experiences with weed/flowers right in our backyard. We do not have a lawn and instead are trying to keep the landscape as natural as possible. Some of the soil that was disturbed during construction has produced a good crop of several kinds of thistle. We chop out the Canada and bull thistle because we don't like the prickly foliage, but we leave the sow thistle because of its pretty yellow flowers. Right outside our kitchen window is a mullein plant. We know it's a weed, but we are preserving it because it is the largest one we've ever seen. It is already six feet tall and just beginning to develop a flower spike!

Weeds or wildflowers, whatever we call them, add a great deal of color and beauty to the landscape.

Canoe Hike

I started out for a stroll down our road the other evening with the intent to observe the progress of the season, to check on the wild fruit crop, and perhaps to find something interesting to share. Before I had reached the end of our drive, the deer flies were swarming around my head, and all the pleasure had gone from the hike. I returned home, having observed nothing but bothersome insects! Then I noticed that the breeze was making a nice ripple on the lake and thought that there might be fewer flying pests out on the water.

I launched our aluminum canoe and found that my theory was true. A few deer flies followed from shore, but they soon dropped behind and I had no more insect problem. However I did have a little trouble handling the canoe. I find that going against the wind with only one person in the canoe requires some skill with the paddle. Being away from the insects gave me a chance to relax and enjoy my surroundings.

A great blue heron that had been fishing took off and lumbered down to the far side of the lake. Several small turtles stuck their heads out of the water and watched until I got too close, then dived and swam away.

Both yellow and white water lilies were in bloom. Judging from the amount of vegetation, this must have been a good year for water lilies. Some of the leaves of the white lilies were fourteen to sixteen inches in diameter—the largest I have ever seen. I was amazed also by the size of some of the lily roots floating on the lake. Some were over ten feet long with numerous branches. I have heard that lily roots are good to eat; if that's true, we have a tremendous supply of food in the bottom of our little lake. Usually we see the lily roots only in the spring when they have been pulled up by the break-up of winter ice. I suspect these had blown on shore and now had floated back out on the unusually high water level this summer.

After completing my explorations I laid the paddle across the canoe and let the wind drift me back toward the house. A good canoe moves over the water with very little resistance. The wind moved me along at a pretty good rate, with no effort on my part. I relaxed completely and enjoyed the sight of tree tops against the deep blue sky. As the wind blew me back to the landing, I thought again what a great invention the American Indians had when they developed the canoe. It's the perfect vehicle in which to travel and enjoy the beauty of the north country.

Water Lilies

There are about ninety different species of water lilies that grow in fresh water in various parts of the world, but only five kinds are native to the U.S.

I have noticed that the white water lilies always look fresh and pretty while the yellow ones are often riddled by insect feeding. The reason for this is obvious when one studies their life cycles. While the yellow flower remains above the water until the seeds develop, the white lily is drawn under the surface after only three days of blooming, and its seeds develop under water.

The seeds of the yellow lily are spread by the bursting seed pod, which throws seeds out into the surrounding area. This gives the plant one of its common names, Spatterdock. The seeds of the white variety develop buoyant seeds coverings, called arils, which float them away from the parent plant. Both varieties also spread by means of their fleshy root stalks.

Unlike land plants, which may suffer from lack of water, the water lily must protect itself from too much water by means of a slimy, gelatinous material, which coats the stems and keeps the water out. Both the stems and leaves are filled with air cells to make them float. In cross section these cells have the appearance of styrofoam. The leaf stalks are flexible, allowing the leaves to float on the surface, even when the water rises or falls. The flower stems are stiffer, holding the blossom a few inches above the water's surface.

Water lilies are both beautiful and useful. Many kinds of insects, bees, and beetles feed on the pollen of the flowers. Deer and moose feed on the leaves and stems; moose also eat the fleshy roots. Beaver and porcupine also eat the roots while ducks feed on the seeds. In earlier times the American Indians used the seeds and roots of the yellow lily as food, and the closely related lotus plant is still eaten in Egypt.

One of the most spectacular members of this family of plants is the giant Victoria water lily, found in the Amazon River of South America. Leaves of this species often grow to a diameter of seven feet! The edges of the leaves are turned up to keep out water. They are so buoyant that a small child can sit on one without sinking!

The summer season in our north country is too short to grow these raft-sized giants, but almost every lake, pond, and stream have an abundance of the smaller, but just as spectacular, varieties.

Dragonflies

I went for a little hike around the yard and down the drive just before sunset. I enjoyed it more than any walk I've taken for several weeks, mainly because the mosquitoes were not as numerous as they have been. Perhaps the decrease in these bothersome pests was caused by the cooler weather. I did notice that there were large numbers of dragonflies darting about, and I'm inclined to give them the credit. As they rushed about, they looked like tiny biplanes with shiny metallic green and blue fuselages and gauze-like wings,though they are much more agile than any man-made plane. The way they were swooping and turning, it was obvious that they were catching smaller insects, but I was never able to get close enough to see if they actually caught a mosquito.

Our encyclopedia reports that both the dragonfly and the closely related damselfly can move at speeds up to sixty miles per hour. Their front legs are lined with a row of bristles, which form a sort of basket for scooping up small insects in flight. The captured prey is eaten on the wing, and each of the aerial acrobats consumes large numbers of flies, gnats and mosquitoes each day.

Not only do the adults of the species benefit us by destroying insect pests, but their nymphs perform a similar service in our lakes and streams. Dragonfly eggs are laid in the water or on waterweeds. These hatch into ugly-looking water insects which spend one to five years preying on water bugs before emerging as winged adults.

The dragonfly goes by many other names and some of them indicate the fear and superstition with which this insect is often regarded. It is variously called devil's darning needle, horse stinger, mule killer and snake feeder. I can remember being told as a youngster to watch out for them because they would sew my ears shut if they landed on my head. Actually there is no reason to fear them at all: they are dangerous only to insects smaller than themselves. Perhaps the superstitions originated in the dryer areas of the country where they are found only around lakes and streams and are not well known throughout the area as they are here.

I'm not sure how much they actually reduce the mosquito population. There are reports that indicate that some of the South Pacific islands would be uninhabitable were it not for the mosquito control effected by several species of dragonflies. If they help at all to reduce the mosquito population, I'm all for them!

August

I have mixed emotions about August. My feelings are still colored by my early years on an old-fashioned farm in central Minnesota. In those days we cut the small grain, wheat, oats, and barley, with a grain binder. We set the bundles into shocks by hand to protect them from the weather until time for threshing. Shocking grain was the hottest, dirtiest job of the whole year!

Making a good shock was something of an art. It required picking up two bundles, one in each hand, and setting them upright so that they would support each other. Then additional pairs of bundles were added to make a shock of eight or ten bundles. If the shocks were to remain in the field for several weeks, a cap bundle was spread over the top to shed rain and protect the grain heads from being eaten by birds.

Shocking grain was heavy work and the dust and chaff added to our discomfort. Shocking barley was the worst. Some of the barley beards always came loose and found their way up our shirts. There is really nothing more irritating than a sticky barley beard!

Today August is still grain harvest month, but much of the hand work has been replaced by machines. The rows of grain shocks no longer dot the landscape even though grain fields at harvest are still attractive. The golden carpet of ripened grain is often cut with a swather and laid in windrows that form concentric patterns of gold on the fields.

Harvest on our north country farms really begins with the first cutting of hay in June and continues until all of the corn is picked in late October or early November. In August wild strawberries are already gone. Blueberries and wild raspberries are at their peak, though the crops are poor in our immediate area. Chokecherries and blackberries will be ready later in the month; both look promising. Garden harvest goes on from the first spring radish to the last fall squash, but August brings us two of my favorites, sweet corn and tomatoes.

The end of the first week in August marks the middle of summer, though most of us think of summer as the school vacation months of June, July, and August. On that schedule two-thirds of summer is gone and the end of the month will mark the end of the season. It's the time for county fairs and the big state fair. There are only a few weeks left for family vacation trips, and then back to school once more.

I still think of August as the hottest month of the year, though that is often not the case. Late August can bring us cool, misty rains and nights that make us think about starting up the furnace. By the end of the month we'll be talking about the feel of autumn in the air and watching ash and birch trees begin to show their fall colors.

Summer Winds

On nearly all of our summer hikes we have been accompanied by the wind. Occasionally in the early evening we have had periods of calm when the surface of the lake showed unwavering reflections, but this season has had more heat and wind than usual.

Summer without wind would be almost unbearable. The wind drives away the stifling heat of dead air, discourages hordes of summer insects, and cools our homes for restful summer sleep. Besides these obvious benefits the wind brings us the sounds and scents of the season, sensations almost unnoticed, without which the summer would be flat and uninteresting.

Summer really begins not with a date on the calendar, but with a sound; the sound of thunder and the patter of the heavy raindrops of a summer storm. Its arrival is confirmed by a pleasant odor—the sweet elusive scent of the wild rose.

The wind brings signals to our senses that give depth and feeling to our visual images. There are sounds like the rattling of aspen leaves in the breeze, waves lapping the shore, and the cry of a loon through the open windows. On hot days the wind brings afternoons filled with the rasping drone of cicada and evenings filled with the rattle of June beetles against the screens.

Odors too come in great variety. A skunk airing his displeasure sends a signal that cannot be ignored. The essence of clover curing in the sun may cause us to smile without conscious effort. A hot afternoon is permeated with the resinous perfume of pine. Some of the farmland scents are more subtle. A rapidly growing corn field has a moist, earthy smell that is hard to describe, but unmistakable to those who know it. At harvest time a field of ripening grain has a faint, musty, straw-like odor.

Sometimes the sounds and odors come together, like the sharp crack and gunpowder smell of firecrackers, or the roar and fumes of an auto race. One of the most refreshing combinations is the soft drumming of raindrops on dry earth followed by the clean fresh smell of rain-washed air.

Soon we will awake to the misty rain of a September morning, and then to the bright golden days of October. Duck hunters' shotguns will punctuate days, and evenings will be filled with the smell of burning leaves. The winds of summer will give way to the breezes of autumn. The wind blows and the seasons roll and the best time of the year is at hand.

Rainbows

Let's talk about rainbows. We can't make a date to go out and search for them; we have to wait until the weather is right to bring them to us, but still they are worth looking for.

Rainbows are even hard to talk about. Phrases like "light refractions" and "component colors" don't really mean very much when no rainbow is visible. Even naming the colors doesn't do it justice. I never could tell where the indigo leaves off and the violet begins. The whole concept of colored light without any physical object to support the pigment is hard to understand; maybe that's why we're always fascinated by rainbows.

We had a rainbow last week that was the most spectacular I've ever seen. It was during the time that Hurricane Allen was moving in toward the Gulf of Mexico. I don't know if that storm pattern affected the weather this far north, but there were some violent thunder and hail storms just to the south of us. We had a great deal of thunder and lightning too, but only brief showers of rain. After one of those showers I happened to glance out a window, noticed a rather bright rainbow, and called it to the attention of the family. Our daughter Carla went outside for a better view and hollered for us to come out. It was a double rainbow, two adjacent bands of spectrum colors. Then for a few seconds it was triple! I thought my eyes were playing tricks on me, but Carla saw it too. Then way above the rainbow in a wider arch was another rainbow with the colors reversed. It didn't last long, but it was a thrilling visual spectacle.

Years ago I remember having seen a bright rainbow in the west early in the morning. We were on our way out for an early fishing trip. It should have been a warning, but we had a good-sized boat, so we went out in spite of the approaching storm. We were literally blown off the lake! The waves ran so high that, when we beached the boat, it filled with water and settled to the bottom in the shallow water.

I've thought since that Rainbow in the Morning would be a good book title. Most of our weather moves from west to east and we see most of our rainbows in the east. This means that when we see a rainbow, the storm is usually past. Most people, whether from experience or from biblical reference, think of a rainbow as a sign of peace and serenity. On the other hand a rainbow in the morning is a sign of approaching violence, a warning that should be heeded. May all of your rainbows be evening benedictions!

A couple of weeks ago our daughter Chris and grandsons Neal (22 months) and Alan (3 1/2 years) came to visit for a long weekend. We had just gotten our pop-up pickup camper, which I set up for the family to admire, and Alan was particularly interested. Somehow I was trapped into agreeing that he and I should sleep out in the camper Saturday night. I had made a remark about Alan and I going camping someday. That was enough for Alan to decide which bed he wanted that very evening. After some coaxing his mother agreed. Alan had been camping several times before, but always in the same tent with his parents.

Immediately after supper, Alan said, "Grandpa, why don't we go out to the camper and go to bed?" Chris pointed out that it was really too early to go to bed, but that argument had no effect, and the invitation to sleep out was repeated about every five minutes. This was an unusual situation; Alan had a long nap that afternoon and it should have taken until at least 10 PM before he was tired. We used some delaying tactics, like a long bath and much reading aloud of bedtime stories, but by 8 PM Alan was in his pajamas and ready to go. I postponed things a bit longer with a bedtime snack and a long shower, but by 9 PM Alan and I were snuggling down in our sleeping bags.

Things were quiet at first. We listened to crickets chirping and a whippoorwill's call, and the sounds of our pup Farley settling down on the tailgate right outside the camper door. Then there was a sort of lonely silence until Alan started a long and profound conversation.

"Grandpa, what if a bear comes?"
"Farley will bark and scare him away."

"What if the bear scares Farley away?"
"Then I'll yell at him, 'Go away, bear!'"

"Grandpa, what if the bear doesn't go away?"
"Then I'll get my gun and shoot the bear."

"Grandpa, what would you do next?"
"Then we could eat the bear."

"But the bear wouldn't be cooked!"
"I would cook him before we ate him of course."

"Grandpa, what if you didn't have any matches to light the stove?"
"Oh, you know I always have matches—to light my pipe."

"But, Grandpa, what if you ran out of matches and didn't have any money to buy some more?"

"Then I would borrow some money from Alan."

"But what if I didn't have any money either?"

"Then we wouldn't eat the bear. But I don't think there are any bears
  around here tonight anyway. Why don't we try to sleep now?
    Goodnight, Alan."

"Adios, amigo!" (The kid must be above average intelligence—
                    he already knows two words of Spanish!)

There was some talk about sleeping out again the next night, but I had to put the top
down on the camper to be ready for work the next morning. Saved by the bell!

Northern Lights

On the same night as a partial lunar eclipse we went out to look at the moon, riding high in the southeast, and were distracted in the opposite direction by the brilliance of the Northern Lights. This was the first good display that I've seen in more than a year. They are awe-inspiring to watch and difficult to describe. These shifting patterns of light seem so far removed from reality that words seem inadequate; only by making comparisons with things more familiar can we approach an accurate description.

On a good night the lights change in shape, intensity, and color even while we watch them. Sometimes they are indistinct, like floating, shimmering, iridescent veils; sometimes they form in solid patterns, like moving curtains of light. Sometimes they appear as separate rays with dark shadows between, rather like sunlight sparkling through a forest of tall, dark spruce trees. On occasion they surround us, coming from east and west as well as north, almost covering the sky. Once I noticed a huge, dark shadow shaped like a mountain (perhaps a cloud) with pinkish fringes of Northern Lights coming from behind like a pale sunrise.

I asked each member of our family to describe the lights, and they too made comparisons. Chris was feeling poetic, or perhaps reverent, and said they looked like falling angel hair. Carla said they looked like searchlights or a halo around the earth. Kathy thought they looked like sun rays through the clouds after a storm. My wife Doris, after commenting that she knew her observation wouldn't show a proper spirit of awe, said that they looked like the opening of a new filling station!

On the occasion of the most recent display I had to drive into town late at night. While in town I looked for the Northern Lights and couldn't see them. The streetlights reflected in the light haze. The moon was visible, but the Northern Lights were not. When I returned home, there the lights were again, a gauze curtain with stars twinkling through.

I am not trying to discourage the use of streetlights, which are an absolute necessity. It is a sad commentary though when our society has progressed to the point where a majority of our population cannot see and enjoy the extraordinary beauty of the Northern Lights on a summer night.

Golden Days

Let's just walk down a country road and absorb the beauty of the golden days of late summer. Almost any road will show us splashes of gold on the landscape. Hay fever sufferers may not share our appreciation of this year's bumper crop of goldenrod, but it does give a decorative look to the roadsides. Wild sunflowers are at their peak now. Their bright yellow flowers are accent points in the patches of dusky goldenrod. In some places the gold has purple splotches of fireweed or wild aster for contrast.

Out in the farming areas the golden landscape persists. Much of the grain crop has already been harvested, but the yellow stubble remains on the fields. Uncut meadows and under-grazed pastures show tall grasses with maturing seed heads that have a soft gold tint, especially in the evening light. Even the bright green corn fields are capped with a coppery blanket of tassels.

Most spectacular of all are the occasional fields of sunflowers. All of the saucer-sized blossoms face the same direction and, when we approach from that side, the view is almost breathtaking. Sunflower production in Minnesota is down from what it was a few years ago, but there are still some large fields in the western part of the state where the golden flowers seem to stretch clear to the horizon.

It's too early for autumn color here, but still our woodlands are showing tinges of gold. In our neighborhood there are some large areas of forest that have been cleared and replanted to pine. The new pines are still hidden in the brush and weeds. Right now the planted areas are almost completely covered with goldenrod. Leaves on the hazel brush are bright green, but the husks of the ripening nuts are beginning to dry, giving the bushes a rusty tinge. Leaves on both ash and birch are beginning to yellow—not enough to call it fall color—but these species have changed enough so that we can pick them out from the green canopy on wooded hillsides.

Besides the changes in foliage color there has been a subtle transition in the quality of sunlight. There is a light haze in the air, probably caused by dust or pollen particles. The sky no longer shows the bright blue of spring or early summer. Instead there is a silvery cast to the sky and the sunlight has a mellow, diffused appearance. Shadows are less dense and sunlight less glaring. Our weather is beginning to cool a bit from the earlier heat waves and insect populations are much reduced. It's a good time to get out and enjoy the golden days!

Sunday Stroll

Recently I renewed an old habit by walking down to the county road to pick up our Sunday paper. The whole trip is only about a mile. Nothing spectacular happened along the way and yet I found it to be a very satisfying hike. For many years this short walk was a part of nearly every Sunday morning and that short stretch of road has become a sort of stage where I watch the passing seasons.

In the spring I observe the beginning of a new year in the world of nature. As the snow melts and the sun becomes warmer, tree buds begin to swell. Tiny leaves, not really green at first, are pastel tints of the same colors they show so vividly in the fall. I often stop to watch the birds in their migration and perhaps stop to drain a puddle. Later in the season I take a passing inventory of the fruit blossoms which indicate what kind of berry crop the summer will bring.

Summer brings relaxing hikes in the cool of the morning. Almost every week the roadside flowers change as summer progresses from wild rose to goldenrod. As autumn approaches I begin to look for deer tracks and guess the size of a buck by the depth and width of the hoof print. I often look up as ducks flash by on whistling wings, or the honk of wild geese draws my eyes to a wedge-shaped formation pointed south. Sometimes I make the whole trip in a sort of trance, completely dazed by the beauty of the autumn foliage.

Winter trips to the paper box are often hurried ones to keep blood circulating to numbed fingers and toes. My old parka is drawn tight around my head, especially on the return trip with the north wind blowing in my face. Some days are nice enough, though, to pause and listen to the raucous call of a non-migrating crow or the lonely questions of an owl in the woods. Little black-capped chickadees seem happy and friendly in any kind of weather.

During the past six months I have largely neglected this old Sunday hiking habit. I get enough physical exercise on my job and don't feel the need for an extra hike on the weekend. Sunday last week was cool with temperatures in the 60's after a very hot week. There were a few deer flies buzzing about, but nothing like the swarms I encountered in July. It seemed good to walk the old familiar track again and I'm going to renew the habit. A leisurely hike with time to watch the progress of the seasons is a good way to begin each new week.

Fall

September Song

Turning the page on the calendar doesn't change the world of nature, but for those of us who live in the north country, there is a psychological change. Labor Day is the end of summer. September is a time of change—no longer summer but not quite autumn either. It's a time when we want to sing the praises of the world of nature.

September is cool, foggy mornings. It's a pair of fishermen depending on a compass and depth finder when the fog is too thick to see landmarks. September is a boy on his way to school with light, misty rain in his face and a frog in his pocket. It is a squirrel hoarding this year's meager crop of acorns.

September is maples and sumac trying to rush the season by showing splashes of red. It is whole ash trees turning to gold as fall really begins. This year should settle the old argument as to whether frost is needed to cause the leaves to change color. This season's foliage began to change before we had temperatures even close to freezing.

Season's change is evident in other parts of our landscape too. Corn, soybeans and sunflowers are all showing signs of maturity. Frequent rains have kept lawns green, but out in the country grasses are showing mature seed heads with tan and yellow tints. Big bluestem, one of our native grasses, is showing its usual rosy-purple color. In some places clumps of this plant are six feet tall.

Most of our song birds are gone. We are beginning to notice the blue jays, chickadees, and nuthatches that have been here all summer. September is ducks in a small flock, taking off from the beaver pond in alarmed flight as though someone had told them about the hunting season. We no longer hear the repetitive call of the whippoorwill on our evening hike. Instead we hear the lonely questioning notes of an owl from the depths of the forest. Soon Canada geese will be flying their v-formations as they migrate south.

September brings us wide variations in temperature. On morning hikes a jacket feels good, but afternoons are straw-hat weather. Outdoor work still causes perspiration, but after dark a blaze in the fireplace is welcome.

September is the golden time of year. Every rural road is lined with goldenrod and brown-eyed susans. It isn't just foliage that shows a golden sheen. The quality of sunlight is different. There is a sort of haze in the air, not like morning fog, but a sort of dusty brightness that makes the day seem less glaring and more relaxing. Perhaps it is the large amount of pollen that is responsible for this atmosphere that is different from any other time of year.

September is a good time here in the north country to go out and enjoy!

All Signs Fail

On all of our recent hikes we have spent a great deal of time looking at the sky, hoping to see rain clouds developing. Sometimes we have seen clouds and even felt a drop or two, but the clouds blow on by and leave the parched earth baking in the sun.

It is early evening as I write these words and the cloud cover is so heavy that we have lights on in the house an hour before sunset. All afternoon the dark clouds have rolled across the sky, but only a trace of moisture has fallen. As I look out my window I see the lake's surface mirror-smooth, with only an occasional dimple caused by a falling raindrop.

All signs fail in dry weather says the old adage, and this summer that has been the case. As a boy I learned that when oak trees in the distance have a silvery appearance, it is sure to rain. Like many of the old beliefs, this one has some basic truth. Oak trees are apparently affected by atmospheric pressure, and when the pressure is falling, they show the lighter-colored undersides of their leaves. I guess we shouldn't blame the oaks for making mistakes; even barometers have been of little value in predicting the weather this summer. Even the old poem about evening gray and morning red has been wrong most of the time. I knew an old farmer named Dan Gordon who lived south of Brainerd. Dan hadn't had much formal education, but he was one of the most intelligent men I've ever met. He was a keen observer of many things, including weather. Dan said, "A mackerel sky and a mare's tail bring rain without fail." Through the years I have found this observation to be true. This summer I have noticed that combination of clouds only twice, and in both cases, we did get some light rainfall.

At our house we've tried almost everything to make it rain. We've washed the car, left the tent out, and even had an open roof overnight when we were doing some remodeling. None of these time-tested methods have produced any results.

Many of us tend to lose our perspective when we are involved in a prolonged drought. I can't remember much about the dry years in the mid-'30s, but I do remember that my parents were philosophical about the situation, and we did survive somehow.

I was quite discouraged when I found that nearly all the trees I planted this spring were dead from lack of water. I have been planting trees for over twenty years and never had such a great loss before. I'll play the odds and plant again next spring. My co-workers at the DNR are having a frantic time fighting fires and are very concerned about the coming fall. I understand and sympathize with them, but I know that in a few years nature will have concealed most of the fire scars created this year. Nature has remarkable powers of recovery.

September, 1981   Autumn Night

I took a little hike after dark on the first night of autumn. There was a damp chill in the air, laced with the smell of wood smoke. My predominant feeling was one of quiet.

Quiet is a relative term. There is usually some sound in the world of nature, but much of the noise of summer has ceased. Many birds have started south and the chill of the night air has quieted the insects.

Earlier in the evening, after a day of carpentry work, I sat out on our deck just to rest a bit. For a few minutes I thought I was living in the city. One of the neighbors was working late clearing some land with his bulldozer. Off to the west a shotgun banged—some lucky grouse hunter finally got a shot. The damp air carried the sound of a clattering truck racing down the county road, and someone else crashed the lid on a metal garbage can. Finally things began to quiet down and the sounds that remained were more peaceful. The breeze swirled the yellowing leaves of the aspen trees in our front yard. Down at the beaver pond a duck quacked, and off in the woods an owl began asking his usual question. I was surprised and delighted to hear the whistle of a whippoorwill. We hear them all through the summer, but they had quit calling several weeks ago and I thought they had all gone south. Perhaps they are still in the area, but have stopped proclaiming their territorial rights. It was nice to hear one again, probably for the last time this year.

Red Rover went with me on my walk and so did our cat. I could hear my boots crunching the gravel and occasion sounds from the dog as he trotted through the tall grass in the tree field. A jet went over, but its roar soon faded until I couldn't distinguish it from the wind sighing through the big pines. I stopped on top of the hill just to absorb the night feeling. For several minutes the breeze made the only sound I could hear.

Somehow it seemed that all the noisy rush of summer had passed and a quieter time had begun. When I think about all the things we still hope to get done before winter, I know that fall will be a busy season. We still have house finishing to do and wood to cut and Christmas trees to harvest. With a little time set aside for hunting, the whole fall will be rather hectic. But still, the season has a quieter, more relaxed feeling than summer.

Autumn Rain

Last Sunday was a relaxing day following a rather strenuous trip to the Minnesota State Fair. I sat out in the evening looking over the lake, watching the soft rain making tiny dimples on the water's surface. I realized that I was watching an autumn rain.

Summer rains are usually violent and short-lived, but this one was soft and gentle. It went on all through the afternoon and into the night, sometimes raining moderately, and at other times little more than a mist. It was the kind of rain that refreshes a thirsty land. There was no runoff and not enough water to replace the summer's losses, but it fell so gently that the earth soaked it up like a sponge.

There are other autumn signs in the countryside too. It is too early for autumn color in the trees, but here and there an over-anxious maple is showing tinges of red at the tips of its branches. We have had enough rain throughout the summer that there is no general browning of the grasses, but the brown, red, and purple tints of maturity still show in the fields and swamp lands. Wild rice heads droop in the shallow lakes and streams, and every roadside is colored gold and blue by goldenrod and wild aster.

Even on a sunny day the change is evident. The temperatures may be as high as those of summer, but the air has a hazy appearance and the deep blue skies of summer no longer show through.

The experienced country dweller can even hear the change that is taking place. Crickets still chirp in the evening twilight, but the strident call of tree frogs, so evident in spring and early summer, has been stilled. The whippoorwill no longer whistles in the night; the croak of the great blue heron and the quavering call of the loon may still be heard, but soon these will be replaced by the honk of wild geese wedging their way south.

Squirrels seem more diligent in storing away their winter food and honeybees are almost in a frenzy as they gather the last of the summer's nectar.

Season's change is evident in the activities of humans as well. The change is especially noticeable in the resort areas. Labor Day and the beginning of school mark a definite end to summer holidays. There may yet be pleasant weekends that will bring people to the area for one last fling at summer fun, but the rush of the season has ended.

As I gazed through the misty rain in the deepening dusk I had the feeling that a deer or even a moose might walk out of the woods on the far shore of our little lake. Let the calendar say it's still summer, but there is a feeling of autumn in the air, and autumn is the finest time of year.

First Fire

Instead of our usual outdoor activity, let's just stay in the house and relax in front of a hearth fire. Early autumn is a joyous time to be out in the world of nature when the weather is good. On some of the cool, rainy days we've had recently the fireplace is more attractive.

Mid-September is one of those awkward, in-between times of the year as far as home heating is concerned. It isn't quite cool enough to warrant starting up the furnace. Still the house has a cold, damp, uncomfortable feel with no heat at all. A fireplace fire is the ideal solution. A cheery blaze and a few degrees rise in temperature changes the atmosphere to cozy.

A hearth fire is especially welcome when it is the first of the season. All summer there have been occasional times when the house felt a bit cool, but we knew that a fire would be too warm. Now with the rain falling and the wind blowing we know that the fire will feel good all afternoon, and be particularly welcome in the evening. Starting the first fire of the season is sort of like coming home to an old pal; it has a friendly familiarity that feels good.

Most times the first fire burns well. The available wood is usually left over from last year and has had a chance to become thoroughly seasoned. We were fortunate to have both birch and oak on hand for that first fire. Birch is great for getting the fire started. Birch bark starts to burn instantly and produces enough heat to ignite the other wood. Oak is much slower starting, but lasts a long time and produces a beautiful bed of coals. Dry aspen produces a clean, bright flame but burns up rather quickly. Pine makes a cheery fire but tends to throw sparks, unless the fireplace is well screened.

One of the nice things about a fireplace fire is that someone has to tend it. That might seem like a disadvantage until it is experienced. The fire tender adds more wood from time to time and occasionally uses the poker to rearrange the logs. The tender isn't expected to leave this responsibility to work on fall chores. He can read sporting magazines, watch the football game on TV or even take a short nap and still be occupied with watching and caring for the fire.

Refreshments seem appropriate when relaxing in front of a fire. A crisp, juicy apple is suitable to the season. We often buy a variety called "Fireside." They aren't very good for cooking, but are hard to beat for eating out of hand. A big bowl of buttered popcorn goes well at such times too.

An open fire seems to have very positive psychological effect on people. Both the sight and sound of the dancing flames seem to promote relaxation and release from tension. Have you ever heard of anyone sitting in front of a hearth fire and worrying? A fire on the hearth is a symbol of comfort and well being.

Much of my hiking has been done in our own back yard. I have been industriously shooting holes in bales of straw with my bow and arrows. I must admit that there are a few holes in the building behind the bales too, and I've even spent some time stomping around in the brush along the lake looking for lost arrows. My aim is improving though, and I hope to be ready for the rumored archery season on deer.

The bow I use is a 54 lb. fiberglass model. It was a gift from my coworkers at the University of Minnesota when I left the staff there in 1957. I did some hunting during the first few years after I received it, but had not even tried it out for several years before this summer. I had some sore shoulder muscles after the first few days of practice, but can shoot 40-50 times now without any trouble.

My interest in the sport was revived when it was announced that the firearms season on deer would be closed this year. Another factor was the arrival in town of Larry Tepley, formerly of Bemidji. Larry is an ardent archer and we are making plans to hunt together.

Much of the fun of deer hunting is the anticipation. Planning and preparing for the hunt is almost as enjoyable as the hunt itself. Stalking the animals or waiting on a stand for them to come by is nearly as important to the hunter as the actual shooting. All of these feelings are present in bow and arrow hunting—perhaps more than in rifle hunting. The archer has all the thrill of the hunt, even though the odds against success are rather high. Both Larry and I feel that we have a pretty good chance of scoring if we can get within thirty yards of a deer, although neither of us has ever shot a deer with a bow.

I did get one of my best hunting stories from an archery hunting trip. I went on an early morning outing with "Scut" Gjertson of Brainerd several years ago. I was hunting deer with my bow and Scut was grouse hunting in the same area. Neither of us saw any game until we were in the car on our way home for breakfast. We suddenly spotted a grouse right beside the road. I decided to try for it with my bow. The grouse sat still while I strung my bow and nocked an arrow; I took careful aim and missed the bird by two feet. Still he sat there. My second arrow plunked him right through the middle.
I had used a target arrow for the shot and even though it was right on, the bird was not dead; it began to jump and flap its wings, gliding off down a hill with my arrow sticking out on both front and back. We never did find the arrow or the bird. If you ever see a weather vane flying around in the woods, that shaft belongs to me!

Golden October

A poet, whose name I can't remember, once wrote about *"October's bright blue weather."* I've always admired and often quoted that phrase; it seems so appropriate to this time of year in our north country. Yet on really considering the matter, I think I would describe October's weather as golden rather than blue.

I've been spending the golden days of early October at various tasks, but the weather and the autumn color seem to have an effect on all of them. I finally got started on some writing that I had been putting off. At times it went quite well, and then I would catch myself gazing out the window at the lake and the bright-leaved birch trees on the far shore. In the evenings it became even harder to concentrate as the reflections on the still water doubled the beauty of the scene.

Many evenings and a few afternoons have been spent working out in the yard. The work wasn't really very strenuous, but still I took frequent rests, just sitting and soaking up the beauty of the autumn weather. We've even taken a little time for some hiking just for the sheer joy of being in the woods at this ideal season.

Bright blue is descriptive of the sky at this time of year. It is a deeper shade than we have seen all summer. The general effect of the weather, however, seems to be anything but blue. Blue is a rather cold color. Our temperatures have dropped a great deal from what they were a month ago, but the yellows, oranges, and reds of the foliage lend an appearance of warmth to the landscape.

Most of our days begin on a silver note at this time of year. Fog is common in the mornings and the grasses are usually coated with either dew or frost. Many recent mornings have been cloudy, with the foliage colors somewhat subdued. Often by mid-morning, the sun comes out and turns the day to gold. The gold-coin leaves of birch and poplar flutter in the breeze or sail slowly down to form a tarnished yellow carpet on lawn and road. Maples, depending on variety, are either flaming scarlet, bright orange, or translucent yellow in the sunlight. Oak trees still haven't reached their peak of color, but are beginning to show reddish-bronze tints.

October afternoons are precious gold with even the sunlight seeming to take on substance and becoming part of the autumn landscape.

In the evening the red tones flame in the setting sun, and then turn to dark blood-red as night comes on. The golden leaves that remain on the trees still show their color until the last hint of twilight has faded.

There is a feeling of deep contentment at the end of such a day. We know that soon we will awake to mornings that are cold and crystal-white; but for now it is enough to hope that perhaps tomorrow too will be another golden October day.

Down by the River

Let's stroll down by the river. Any river will do, but a small one is best—one too small for commerce or disposal of industrial wastes. The best time is a sunny afternoon in late spring or early fall, when the weather is warm but insects aren't too numerous.

We can hear the sounds of the river even before we see it. Besides the soft gurgle of moving water, the birds, most of them unseen, provide a whole symphony of sound. The meadow lark's sweet liquid notes are accompanied by the chirping of sparrows and the pleasant rasping trill of blackbirds. If we listen closely, we can hear the soft sad whistle of a mourning dove. No summer sound is more melancholy, and yet it makes us feel more relaxed and content than sad.

Let's pick a nice grassy spot on the bank and just sit and enjoy the river. Our eyes are greeted with an ever-changing pattern as the water ripples and swirls by. Gravel and rocks in the swift- moving stream have a clean washed look, and the sandbars have been sculpted into soft waves. We have an almost irresistible urge to go wading. Perhaps that feeling is a holdover from our childhood when going wading meant summertime and free-dom from school. Remember the shock of that cold water and the feeling of sand between bare toes?

In the shallows a few minnows swim. There's a crayfish under the rock's edge. Let's take a stick and see if it will grab it with its claws. No, the crayfish doesn't seem interested in sticks today; it's backing off and moving to a safer spot. We always used to say that a crayfish swims backwards because it wants to see where it's been rather than see where it's going. Probably it's easier to pull those big claws through the water than it would be to push them ahead. The eyes of a crayfish, and most other crustaceans, are on short movable stalks so they can swivel them well in all directions.

The sights and sounds along a river are almost too numerous to remember. A duck flashes by on whistling wings and a kingfisher sits poised on the lowest branch of a tree that's leaning over the water while the green pasture grass forms a backdrop for the whole scene. Besides the things we see and hear, there is a feeling about a river, a feeling of contentment.

At this time of year a day with a northwest wind is likely to provide us with ideal hiking conditions. Weather predictions based on wind direction alone may not be as accurate as the weather bureau forecasts, but a northwest wind is a pretty reliable indicator of clearing skies and cool temperatures.

The hot muggy days that we sometimes get at this season usually have winds out of the southeast or southwest. Southwest winds may blow up a thunderstorm, while the more easterly breezes often bring a slow, steady, prolonged rain. When the weather vane shifts to the northwest we can expect a rising barometer. Within a day or so the whole weather pattern changes and for a time we can enjoy cool, crisp, cloudless autumn weather.

Northerly winds in winter are another matter. They still bring clearing skies, but temperatures may drop to the point where the wind chill makes outdoor activity almost impossible. A north wind in winter is a wolf wind with icicle fangs that symbolize the fiercest cold of the year. Even in spring a northwest wind can chill the blood and take all the joy out of the season. However in summer it blows away the hoards of mosquitoes and other insects, dries up the humidity and makes life in the north country a joy.

In autumn those high pressure days are the best that any year can offer. Dawn on such a day reveals mist hovering over the lakes and the sun rising in a cloudless sky. Every lawn and meadow will soon be coated with a light frost. One can measure the progress of the sun as its warming rays turn the frost to glistening droplets of water on each blade of grass.

As the warmth and wind dry out the night's moisture, the day seems ideal for outdoor activity. I find myself itching to get out the old 12-gauge to go tramping off through the woods in search of ruffed grouse. Such a day seems made-to-order for sitting in a tree stand with bow and arrow, listening for approaching deer. I know that the seasons aren't open yet, but the weather seems right for it. We might paddle the canoe out on a small lake and try for trout. Northwest winds don't always produce the best fishing, but on such a day, fishing can be beautiful even if nothing bites!

Work can be refreshing on this kind of day if it is done out in the open air. We have been spending time trapping gophers on our tree farm and hauling in the winter's wood supply—and enjoying both. Perhaps part of the pleasant feeling comes from knowing that the fall hunting seasons will be more fun if the fall work is already done.

We will have a great variety of weather during the next few weeks. There will be a few more hot, sticky days and some cold, rainy ones. When the wind changes to the northwest, however, get ready to go outdoors and enjoy some of the best days of the north country year!

Nature's Bounty

Those who live on farms or raise large gardens are aware of the abundance of produce at this season, but others tend to forget.

Harvesting has been going on ever since mid-summer. As fall begins nature rushes to complete the ripening of the crops before freezing weather. Apple trees hang heavy with bright red fruit, and even the late-maturing varieties are ripe and sweet. Clusters of grapes show through yellowing foliage. The wild grape crop is poor in our area, but domestic grapes seem to be bearing well.

Squirrels rush about collecting a heavy yield of hazel nuts. Acorns begin to fall from oaks; we have our cars parked under an oak in the back yard and I often hear the acorns bouncing off the roof or hood. Milkweed and other wind-borne seeds sail out on the autumn winds to assure another generation and another harvest.

Personally I am most conscious of the season's generosity in connection with my wine making hobby. Wild cherries, in particular, were plentiful this year. I started a large batch of pin cherry wine and then set up the last batch of wine from our rhubarb patch. This left me with barely enough room to take care of a small part of the chokecherry bumper crop. My friend George McKinzie called, offering more rhubarb. We gladly accepted the gift but put it in the freezer for later brewing. Then Dan Campbell and Ole Howard collaborated to provide us with two bushels of beautiful crab apples. I did manage to get about half of these into fermentation crocks and passed the remainder on to another amateur wine maker. The crab apple wine is into the secondary fermentation stage while we begin picking domestic grapes. It's been a great year for winemaking activity!

Nature's annual cycle of seedtime, growth, harvest, and rest is moving into the fourth and final stage. Autumn's brilliant foliage is the colored bunting for nature's harvest festival. It's a joyous proclamation of the completion of another bounteous year, and a sort of reassurance that all is prepared to guarantee a repeat performance when the cycle begins again next spring.

There is one more harvest to finish for those of us who work with Christmas tree plantations. Tree cutting time will soon be here and then both our final harvest and the calendar year will be complete.

Farley, our golden retriever, and I went for a leisurely Sunday afternoon stroll a week ago. We didn't expect any contact with wildlife, but about half way down the drive we noticed an animal ambling along up ahead. I recognized it as a young porcupine. Farley and I saw the animal at the same time and the dog was ready to attack.

"Farley, no! Farley, come! Farley, heel!" I gave the commands and the dog obeyed at once. We were about a hundred feet from the porky when it left the road and was lost in the tall grass and weeds. I looked at the place where the animal had disappeared, but didn't want to take the chance of following it into heavy cover.

Farley is well trained, but perhaps his prompt obedience was spurred by memories of his previous encounters with porcupines. On two occasions he had come home with a dozen quills in his muzzle. Farley is a very trusting dog and seems to recognize when I am trying to help him, even when the help is painful. I used a pliers to pull out the quills. The dog whimpered at each pull, but didn't try to bite or run away.

I have mixed emotions about porcupines. I have heard it said that porcupines should be preserved as an emergency food source. If someone were lost in the forest they might be able to kill a slow-moving porcupine with a club and its meat might prevent starvation. I talked once with some men who had roasted porcupine over an open fire. They said it was the worst food they had ever tasted.

Some of my forester friends destroy porcupines at every opportunity because of the severe damage they cause to pine trees. Porcupines will often chew off the bark, completely girdling the tree and causing the top to die off. I have seen this kind of damage on our own tree farm.

Our most serious clash with a porky happened a number of years ago. At that time we had a golden retriever called Copper King. One morning I came out of the house and found the dog lying by the back door whimpering softly. His whole face and mouth were studded with quills. Some of the sharp barbs stuck clear through his tongue and into the roof of his mouth. Doris called the vet while I loaded the dog in the back seat of the car. The vet gave Copper King an anesthetic and pulled out over one hundred quills. We were fairly certain that this porcupine had come right into our yard. We later discovered that our daughter's horse had a few quills in her nose.

Porcupines are interesting animals and I wouldn't want to see them eradicated. Their place, though, should be in the deep woods, not in places where they can make contact with children or pets.

Primeval Swamp

I took a little hike the other evening down to the end of the lake. There is a small area there that I like to visit now and then, not so much for what it contains as for what it lacks. Similar places are common throughout the north woods, and for want of a better name I call them "dead" swamps.

They are not really dead of course; like almost all land and water areas they abound with insect and plant life. But these areas do have the appearance of death. The grasses that grow around the edges of these areas, and the stunted bushes that grow out in the center never reach a height of more than two feet. They do grow in great profusion, but at this time of year they have turned to a neutral, brownish color, and to the casual observer appear dead. The soil is apparently too wet and too acidic to support any other plant life. At some time in the past they must have been dry enough for trees to take root and grow for a few years. Now the broken stubs of their trunks and their grotesquely pointing limbs add to the cemetery-like impression which one gets from viewing such a place.

A dead swamp is one of the few areas that has remained unchanged by civilization. It never had any trees worth cutting and is much too wet to plow. It does not contain enough open water to attract ducks or even muskrats. Not even cattle or wild animals use it for pasture. All around the edges the second or third growth timber is vibrant with life; growth and change are always apparent. In the swamp the same dead stubs remain year after year. It's the sort of landscape where one gets the feeling that a dinosaur could appear at any time and not feel a bit out of place.

Small birds do make some use of these areas because the grasses that grow there produce an abundance of seed. Chickadees feed in the fall and early winter, and flocks of warblers stop on their northern migration to gather a few remaining seeds in the spring. Outside of these seasonal visitors the only animal life present is of the most primitive types, represented by frogs and reptiles.

Some of our more fertile swamps are excellent places for observing wild life of many kinds. For me the dead swamp serves a different purpose. At the end of a busy summer it is pleasant to have somewhere to go where one can escape from all signs of civilization. Sometimes a person needs to feel a sense of isolation, a sort of recess from society. Such an interlude makes future contacts with one's fellow man more meaningful and more pleasant.

Wild Geese

My hiking companions and I talked a bit about the thrill of hearing migrating geese late at night. I've been doing some driving in west-central Minnesota, and I've seen numerous flocks of Canada geese in the area. Sometimes they are resting on the small lakes and often feeding in farm fields. They seem particularly attracted to small grain that has been windrowed but not yet combined. I have noticed several such fields with large flocks feeding and numerous smaller groups flying in to attend the banquet.

I suspect that many of the geese are a part of the Fergus Falls flock. A goose refuge was established there several years ago. The number of geese in the area has increased each year. Now the population is so high that it is becoming a nuisance.

Apparently some of the romance associated with with geese diminishes if you live on one of the city lakes and have your front yard covered with geese for most of the year. Farmers,who have part of their crops destroyed by geese, tend to lose their affection quickly. I have heard that some of the landowners near refuges make more money from renting hunting spots than they do from farming. I've only been goose hunting once, but it is a sport that I would like to try more often.

I have a special sort of feeling about wild geese. The honking flock in flight calls up visions of the lonely and remote areas of the far north where most of them spend their summers. Wild geese are the heralds that proclaim the season's change. When we see their v-formations on northward migrations, we know that there is open water and that spring has really arrived. Their fall flights tell us that the season is changing and that it's time to prepare for winter. These big birds are the symbols of wildness and freedom. They let us know that there are still some remote spots left where humans have not destroyed their habitat.

Hitchhiking

I hadn't tried hitchhiking for 20 years until last month, and I'm still amazed at the success I had.

I had been moose hunting in northern Saskatchewan with a party of four. We had spent a week in the bush (a Canadian expression for woods) without even seeing a moose. My companions decided to move to a different area, further south, and to hunt for another week. I had commitments to keep so decided to return home by bus. I caught the Grey Goose at The Pas, Manitoba, and rode all through a rainy night, arriving in Winnipeg about 7 AM.

I missed the southbound bus by about two minutes, and was informed that there would not be another until 5:30 PM. Winnipeg is a lovely city, but I did not relish the thought of spending the whole day there. Another line had a bus to International Falls, but no connections going south, so that wasn't much help. I had done a lot of hitchhiking when I was in military service and in college, and found it a pleasant and inexpensive way to travel. I really wondered though if anyone would pick up a man wearing blue jeans and a slightly soiled hunting coat. I figured I couldn't lose much by trying, so I used a dressing room at the bus depot to shave and clean up, took a taxi to the edge of town, and stuck out my thumb.

My first ride was in a rendering company truck, the kind used to pick up dead animals for salvage. The odor wasn't too bad if the window was open. The driver was heading for the U.S. border crossing to pick up a dead pig that had been left at the inspection station there. That got me to and across the border, but I found myself on the freeway leading into North Dakota rather than on Highway 75 in Minnesota as I had intended. There are two border stations within a couple of miles of each other, and I had crossed at the wrong one. A kindly gentleman who worked at the border station went a couple of miles out of his way on his lunch break to get me back on the right road. I hadn't been out on the highway more than five minutes when a big semi-truck stopped to give me a lift. The driver had hauled a load of fruit into Winnipeg and was running empty to Moorhead, Minnesota, to pick up a load for the East Coast. This wasn't the most direct route home, but it was too good a chance to pass up.

From Moorhead a series of six short rides brought me in to Brainerd, only about twelve hours after I had left Winnipeg. I got home sooner than I would have if I had made my bus connections in the morning! I met a number of interesting people; several of them commented that my hair was shorter than most hitchhikers' they saw these days. My fastest ride was between Detroit Lakes and Perham with three young swingers in a purple sports car; quite a contrast from the dead animal truck! I'm still marveling at the kindness and generosity of today's motorists.

Floating Leaves

Our best hike last week was a noon lunch on the banks of the Crow Wing River. There wasn't a lot of wildlife moving that day. There was a muskrat swimming against the current, a family of nine ducks feeding in the shallows, and a big hawk sailing up the river valley. The highlight of the day, though, was the autumn leaves floating on the water.

This is the time of year for leaves to be falling; there is nothing unusual in that. Somehow though I had never before really looked at leaves floating on a river current. Perhaps I was attracted by the large numbers of them. A short distance upstream from my lunch spot, a number of maple trees hung out over the water. Each of them was showering yellow leaves on the moving water. The leaves floated with the current, causing interesting patterns on the river's surface. The day was bright and sunny, and the leaf patterns were repeated in shadows on a sandy stretch of river bottom.

My attention was caught by the large numbers of maple leaves, but as I watched, I was able to identify the leaves of several other tree species. There were long, slender willow leaves, and sharply pointed red oak leaves. Ash, two kinds of aspen, ironwood and alder all contributed to the moving patterns.

My first feeling was that the leaves, like our summer birds, were migrating south for the winter, but I knew that these particular leaves would never be coming back. They were leaving their forest home for good. It was as though the glory of our autumn woodlands was being carried away by the river. The whole process seemed sort of sad. Then I noticed that leaves were collecting in every eddy caused by rocks and other obstructions in the current. In some spots leaves were stuck on weeds and submerged logs on the river bottom. The leaves weren't really leaving the north country. They were just taking a short ride on the current until they became waterlogged and sank.

All in all, the scene on the river was one of beauty and peace. Sunshine warmed the air that had been near freezing in the morning. Only a few fluffy white clouds floated in a deep blue sky, making the blue seem more intense. I had only an hour in which to try to absorb all that beauty, and I really wanted more.

A good-sized fish splashed in the shallow water not far from shore. I wished then that I could be in a boat fishing instead of just having lunch on the bank. It would have been an ideal time to spend the whole day drift-fishing the river, even if the fish weren't biting. It would have been enough just to spend the sun-warmed hours savoring the beauty along the banks and on the water.

Hiking with a Dog

I sometimes think that we should change the heading for these columns to "Hiking with Farley." Farley is our half-breed golden retriever, our constant companion on all of our outdoor activities.

The dog is ten years old, but when I come out the door and call his name, he acts like a pup. He dances in circles and snuffles my hand, hoping to get his ears scratched. He follows close beside me, his wagging tail banging against my leg.

Our most frequent hike is down our half-mile driveway to the mailbox. We go out to mail letters, pick up the mail, or just for exercise. After a minute or so of prancing around Farley moves out to act as advance scout. He trots back frequently to make sure that I am still coming. He sniffs briefly at tracks where a pair of deer have crossed the driveway. He learned long ago that it doesn't pay to chase deer. He picks up other scents where there is no sign that my weak senses can discover. Farley stops to pick berries along the way. All of the summer fruits are gone, but he has developed a taste for rose hips. He just has to ingest a few of these bright red fruits on each walk.

We have trained the dog to sit and stay when we near the end of the drive. We wanted to be sure that he wouldn't run out on the blacktop in front of a passing car. This stop has become routine and the dog does it now without command. Once released from the "sit" and "stay," Farley has to leave his scent marks at the driveway's end just so other canines will know that they are trespassing on his territory.

As I return to the house the dog often lags behind, as though he didn't want the trip to end. He makes forays into the Christmas tree plantation that borders the drive. Sometimes he stops to dig for a gopher. Occasionally he actually digs one out, usually in early summer when the half-grown gophers have not yet learned to dig deeply. When this happens, the dog comes trotting proudly, bearing his trophy in his mouth.

Our autumn days are so busy that I seldom get out for grouse hunting. On the rare occasions when I do hunt, the dog recognizes the shotgun and is more eager than ever to go with me. The grouse population in our area has been quite low for several years. I often do not fire a shot on these short hunts, but still there is a special camaraderie between the hunter and his hunting dog that seems very special to both of us. It's the hunt, not the game that is important.

A well-trained dog is a near-ideal hiking companion. The dog is always eager to be out and that enthusiasm is contagious. The hunting dog never argues. He only complains when in pain, like having a sand burr in a paw. Being out with a dog is good therapy for anyone.

Fall Bird Watching Time

Late fall is a good time for bird watching. Birds are not as numerous as they are in summer, but with most of the leaves gone from the trees, they are easier to see.

I still notice an occasional robin in the area, but most of the birds have already flown south. Those that nest farther north are passing through, and we are seeing species that we haven't seen since they came north last spring. One morning last week we had a whole backyard full of slate-colored juncos. Apparently traveling with them were a few small birds with light yellow patches, which I believe were immature warblers. One disadvantage to fall bird watching is that many of this year's hatch do not yet have their mature colors, making them harder to identify. Occasional horned larks come through too, but are much less conspicuous than in spring.

We have put out our sunflower seed feeder again and are getting reacquainted with our winter birds. The feeder was out for four days before the birds discovered it; now the chickadees and nuthatches are feeding regularly. We are pretty sure that some of these are the same individuals who were here last winter because a couple of the nuthatches had developed a habit of placing sunflower seeds in a small hole in our deck railing to peck off the hulls. This same behavior is being repeated this fall and I believe it unlikely that a new bird would have discovered this trick so soon.

The feeder we use is designed for small birds. It has short perches right below each hole where the seeds are available. Larger birds, such as the evening grosbeaks, find it difficult to remain on the perch and reach the seeds. We like this arrangement because we don't think we can afford the amount of sunflower seeds that would be required to feed all the grosbeaks in the neighborhood! This year one of our resident blue jays has figured out a way to remain on the perch by bracing himself with his tail while swallowing sunflower seeds, hulls and all.

We are certain that some of our feeding birds are new to the area. Recently we've seen what appears to be a mutant chickadee. The bird's size, shape, and actions are the same as other chickadees, but it lacks the familiar black cap. Instead its entire head is covered with white plumage. When I first noticed this individual I thought that it was carrying a white feather that covered its head, but when it came closer to our kitchen window, we could see that its head feathers were pure white. We hope this little fellow stays around; it's nice to have one bird that is easy to identify!

The other evening on my way home from work I encountered a flock of snow buntings along the road. Usually we don't see them until winter snows are covering the whole landscape. I hope that wasn't a sign of early winter. Perhaps they were reminding us to get out and enjoy the variety of the fall bird migration now. Soon our winter birds will be all that remain here.

Why Hunt?

On our hike today let's carry a shotgun. That makes our hike into a hunt. All of us know the virtues of hiking, but how about hunting? There is a great deal of anti-hunting propaganda these days; perhaps it's time to consider the motivation for those of us who enjoy hunting.

From an economic point of view most hunting and fishing expeditions are a poor investment. Over the years we have done pretty well on deer hunting near home. We have obtained some excellent quality meat at reasonable cost. On our other sporting endeavors we would be much better off to purchase meat rather than hunt or fish for it. Of course, the return on the investment depends on how we figure. If we consider the recreational value of our outings to be worth the expense, then any game we get is free.

There are, of course, many factors to discuss other than the economic ones. Of prime importance to me, and to many sportsmen, is the fellowship of hunting and fishing. In social situations and at work we are involved with many different types of people, but a hunting companion is selected with great care. A hunting partner is someone to depend on, someone with similar interests who is capable of sharing the joys and disappointments of the chase. A good hunting partner is someone whose success and enjoyment is more important than your own. A relationship like this is rare in normal endeavors, but fairly common in outdoor sports.

Hunting is an activity that promotes self-reliance. In modern society almost everything we use is purchased. In hunting and fishing, as well as in gardening, we have the opportunity to provide something ourselves. Success in hunting gives one a feeling of independence. For a little while we can look at world affairs and say, "I can make it on my own."

There is also a feeling of complete success in taking a limit of game or fish. Most things we do are done "pretty well," but someone else might have done it better. A limit of birds or fish, however, is the best anyone could do legally. This feeling is especially strong in deer hunting where the limit is one deer; any success in this sport is complete success.

Some say that the urge to hunt is a primeval one, carried over from our cavemen ancestors. Success at hunting back then was the difference between plenty and famine. The skillful hunter was the hero and main provider for the clan or family. Our living conditions have changed, but perhaps some of the old instincts remain.

Whether or not one believes in primeval instincts, there is no question that we have a hunting heritage from our pioneer ancestors in this country. As civilization advanced, hunting changed from subsistence to sport, but it has always been considered a good and honorable avocation.

October 16 was opening day for the Minnesota Bow and Arrow Deer Season. I spent most of the day sitting in a tree near a deer trail, with plenty of time for thinking. Perhaps my thoughts were not truly philosophical; a hunter is a little too anxious to think great thoughts, but there was time to wonder about many things. There was time to observe closely the things of nature and to absorb the atmosphere of the forest.

The night before the opening was cold and rainy. Each time I awoke during the night, the rain was pouring down and it still persisted when I got up in the morning. We took warm clothing and rain gear and drove to the hunting area; still the rain came down. Then just before dawn the rain stopped. The woods were still cold and wet, but we moved out to our chosen stands before daylight.

Five of us from Brainerd had decided to hunt an area where deer had been feeding in soybean and alfalfa fields, which were surrounded by heavy woods. I had picked my stand the night before and was able to find it in the dark. Along a main deer trail leading off the fields, a large oak branch had broken and fallen to the ground, providing easy access to a crotch in the tree about ten feet off the ground. An ideal place to wait for deer, and fairly comfortable.

There is a lonely feeling in the cold dark woods, but on opening morning it is colored by anticipation. At first there was nothing to see and the only sound was the water dripping from the trees. The smell of decaying leaves filled the air as I waited for dawn. There really was no "dawn" that morning, just a gradual lightening of the overcast sky, but eventually the tree trunks and bushes took form in the growing light.

One rustling sound that I was sure was a deer turned out to be a pair of gray squirrels in a nearby oak. I watched them most of the morning traveling through the treetops and returning by the same route, carrying something that looked like pine cones.

Once a ruffed grouse nearly landed in my tree, then deflected at the last minute. It landed in another tree close by but had apparently seen me as it seemed very nervous and finally flew off into the woods. A blue jay saw me too, and screamed in a loud voice at the intrusion.

The morning wasn't quite like other deer season openings; it was too quiet. There were a few shots in the distance, shotgunners out for ducks or grouse, but the sharp crack of high-powered rifles was missing. My own feelings were different too. There isn't so much urgency about bow and arrow hunting. The odds against success are much greater, and instead of only a few days, I could look forward to a whole month of hunting.

None of our party saw any deer, but we'll go out again. Even if we get nothing but fresh air, fellowship, and time to think, the experience is worthwhile.

November Is

Here we go hiking into November, a hard-to-predict month. November weather can be pleasant or miserable. We don't always know what to expect, but there are a few things we can be pretty sure of in the eleventh month of the year.

We can be certain that winter will arrive on the land before it arrives on the calendar. One day we will see the ice rimming our lakes, trying to trap the living water into its winter prison. By the next morning the campaign is ended, ice covers the water, and winter reigns once more. On a dark afternoon snowflakes fall like a benediction on the brown-robed earth. Bare trees stand like skeletons, except for the oaks that refuse to release their leaves. We are thankful once more that we live among the pines that hold their needles to dull the cutting edge of the winter winds.

November is the shrieking call of a blue jay, scolding the weatherman. Or is this blue-feathered scamp crying, "Thief—Thief!" at a deer hunter in a tree stand? Those of us who hunt in the northeastern part of the state hope for success early in the season. A full moon on November 14 gives the deer light for feeding at night and a chance to spend the whole day in hiding.

Veterans Day on the 11th of the month is a recognized holiday. For the north country sportsman it means another day for deer hunting without using up vacation time. In the old days the deer hunting season used to run over Thanksgiving Day. I think most wives and mothers prefer the earlier dates. Hopefully hunters will find the earlier dates to be less frigid.

November brings the winter birds to the sunflower seed feeder—birds that we have not seen all summer. Friendly little chickadees will take a seed from our hands if we are patient with them. Nuthatches that go head first down the trunk of a tree, insist at their turn at the feeder. Small woodpeckers are a bit shy, and we only occasionally catch sight of the giant pileated woodpecker. Yellow and black grosbeaks are pretty, but will eat you out of house and home if given the chance. Ruffed grouse that survived the hunting season will come in to the yard to feed on the buds of aspen and ironwood.

November is hauling in fireplace wood, letting it have a chance to dry before being burned to give us a bit of warmth and cheer.

Thanksgiving is one of our best holidays. It has not been commercialized as much as some of the others. We don't have to buy a gift to let our friends and family know how much we appreciate them. With November's uncertain weather we are never quite sure if we will have a white holiday or not. We usually do have some of those white flakes. If nothing else, they help those of us who live in the north country get in the mood for Christmas. Among our many blessings we can give thanks that we live in such a beautiful part of the country.

Fallen Leaves

A week of heavy rain has brought down most of the leaves and leached the color from those that remain. A short time ago the whole woodland was a riot of color—gold, scarlet, orange and maroon. Now only shades of gray and brown remain.

The fallen leaves are pleasant underfoot and while walking down a woods trail, I have an almost irresistible urge to scuff my feet just to hear the leaves rustle. Of course there are still variations of color to be seen. The carpet of leaves on the forest floor is not a solid color but a tweed. The oak leaves are shiny, bronze-like brown while the aspen leaves are faded to a dull gray. Here and there are spots of brighter color; tufts of green grass show through the leaf mat and some small bushes still cling to red or yellow leaves. In the more shaded areas tiny wintergreen plants are bright and shiny, oblivious of the season's change. Their red berries are the brightest spots of color we will see until spring.

This is the season when birch and pine seem to come into dominance in the woodland scene. The snow-white trunks of birch contrast sharply with the duller colors of the other hardwoods and brush. The pines not only maintain their everlasting soft, green color so pleasant to the eye, but the ear too again detects their presence. Wind through a pine grove has a distinctive sound at any time of the year, but it is much more noticeable when the other trees are bare.

I always feel a tinge of melancholy each autumn when the leaves fall, and at the same time a sense of pleasant anticipation of the season to come. The loss of leaves improves the visibility in the woods and should make for better grouse hunting. The falling of the leaves is like the drawing aside of a curtain that has hemmed us in all summer. In heavy brush areas the woods can be almost oppressive during the season of rank summer growth. After the leaves fall the woodsman has a clean, clear vista that is refreshing to the mind. Looking through the woods a few weeks ago our range of vision was limited to a few feet, while now a birch trunk a hundred yards away stands out sharp and clear. Now we feel that there is a good chance to see the deer and other game that, during the summer, had moved through the woods as though invisible.

The season of fallen leaves is evident in the yard as well as in the forest. Lawns are almost obscured by the covering of brown. Children seem unable to resist the urge to rake up huge piles of leaves. Not that they are intent on cleaning the yard; it's just that it's so much fun to jump into a heap of leaves.

Deer Hunting

This week let's go deer hunting.

A great deal of the fun is anticipation. It begins immediately after the close of one season, and leads up to the beginning of the next. Those who think that deer hunting is a sport only ten days each year, don't know deer hunters. All those stories about the deer seen and killed and the excuses for the shots missed—they're all part of the mental preparation for next year's season. There is always the hope that it will happen the same way again, only next time the shot will be true to the mark.

As the season draws nearer the anticipation takes the form of preparation. Red clothes are dug out from the mothballs, compasses checked, and new socks purchased. Hunters' wives get involved in the deer season fever too, with purchase of extra groceries, lunch making, and a dozen other little preparatory chores. There are rifles to sight-in, ammunition supplies to check, and hunting territory to look over before opening day arrives.

During the last week before the season, most hunters are hoping for snow. Snow cover probably has little effect on the number of deer taken, but it does make it easier to locate areas in which deer have been moving. It also improves the visibility in the woods—and the thing most important to many sportsmen—it makes it possible to be sure that no seriously-wounded game will be lost.

One of the most pleasant parts of preparation for hunting is the planning that takes place between members of the hunting party. The choice of hunting companions is an extremely important decision. During recent years I have noticed that a very large proportion of hunting accidents are either self-inflicted or are caused by someone within the hunting party. Deer hunting, with the right companions, is probably safer than driving a car on the public highway.

On opening morning the anticipation reaches its peak. The very early rising, the extra-nourishing breakfast, and the meeting with hunting buddies before dawn all add to the expectation. Many hunters like to be in the woods and on the stand while it is still dark so as not to frighten off any game that may be moving into the area at dawn. As the sun rises the suspense increases— any sound in the woods might be an approaching deer. The feeling is so exciting and so intense that deer hunting is a great sport, even on those days when no deer are killed.

Little Leaves

Some of our nature hikes produce exciting adventures that we can share with others. Some of them are rather uneventful. Invariably though there are some little things that catch our interest. One day last week I was intrigued by the discovery of some little leaves.

It was one of those days when I was scheduled to spend the whole day at my desk. On such days I usually carry my lunch and drive down to the river during noon hour. After a sandwich and coffee I take a short hike down the riverside road. This particular day was cloudy, damp and cool. The brilliant color of autumn maples was gone and even the oak leaves had turned a dull, rusty brown. I saw no wildlife except for a few chickadees. The air was filled with the odor of decaying leaves. I like that smell of autumn, and it felt good to be out walking in the woods even for those few minutes.

I noticed some fresh deer tracks on the road. As I was examining them I saw a tiny burr oak leaf. It was brown and dried like all the other fallen leaves, perfectly formed, but only about an inch long. A few yards farther down the trail, I found another one about the same size. I have them on my desk as I write these words and they seem rather special. They don't have any particular value except that they represent something that I had never seen before. I expect to see small leaves in the spring but not in the fall. Perhaps this is something that occurs every year but I had not noticed it.

I mentioned my find to an acquaintance who informed me that the larger leaves grow at the top of the tree in full sunlight, and the smaller ones lower down in the shade. I checked the burr oak that grows next to our garage and found that the leaves varied from about two to six inches in length, but this tree had no one inch miniatures, perhaps because it was not shaded by other trees.

I find that preparing these weekly columns has some beneficial by-products for me. One of them is that I am more observant than I used to be. It's quite common to look at things in the world of nature without really seeing them. There is an old story about a college biology professor who decided to go on a trip during his summer vacation. He vowed that he would stop and examine every plant, animal, and insect that he found along the way. By the end of the summer he had traveled nearly halfway across his back yard!

It is true that the world of nature offers us an almost infinite variety. There is always something of interest if we take the time to really see our surroundings. Even things like little leaves can cause a sense of wonder.

Last Harvest

It's harvest time! Harvest time is six months long here in Minnesota. From the first cutting of hay in June until the last of the corn and sunflowers in November, it's always time for some kind of harvest. Now, however, we've come to the end of the season and there is a rush all through the countryside trying to finish the work before winter begins.

During the last couple of weeks we have been a part of this harvest rush. It's Christmas tree harvest time too. No, it isn't too early to cut Christmas trees. Our plantation is all pines, and pines hold their needles and keep their fresh appearance for several months. If the weather should turn unseasonably hot, there could be some drying of the needles, but we pile the cut trees to reduce exposure and prevent drying. From the grower's point of view there is less chance of hot, drying weather than there is of heavy snow. We know from previous years' experience that deep snow can make tree-cutting very difficult.

Even with ideal weather, cutting trees is strenuous work. A day of sawing, dragging, baling and loading wears me out. I suspect that part of the problem is increasing age, but some of our younger workers complained almost as much as I did. Our tree business isn't large enough to be very mechanized. We cut some of the trees with a Swede saw and some with a small chain saw. We drag them out to the firebreaks by hand and pull them through a baling funnel by hand too. The baling is the most strenuous part of the job except when we are loading large trucks and have to throw the trees to the top of a stock rack. Still, if the weather isn't too bad, it is enjoyable outdoor work.

At our former home we used to harvest quite a number of trees in December when people would come to select their own tree from our plantation. That was especially enjoyable when families with children came. The kids would run around the field, shouting, "Here's one, Daddy!" "Here's another one, Daddy!" "I want this great big one!" "Daddy, could we get a little one for my room?" It was a good time to renew friendships with people that we might see only once a year.

I remember that the time it took to select a tree was inversely related to the temperature. On a nice day it might take nearly half an hour to find the perfect tree, but when a cold wind was blowing, the selection could be made in three minutes. It will be several years before the trees we've planted on our new farm will be large enough to sell in this way.

This year we have trees going out in all directions. Trees we raised will be on sale in Brainerd, Pine City, St. Paul, East Grand Forks, Moorhead, Slayton and Omaha, Nebraska. It's fun to think about all of the families who will be decorating them next month.

November Gray

Our hikes have lost their vibrant color. The scarlet and gold has been replaced by shades of gray and dull, lifeless brown. Here and there a patch of tamarack retains its golden glory, but gray predominates.

If I were a landscape artist painting an early November scene, I would do it in shades of gray, for this time of year seems gray in spirit as well as in hue. There is a melancholy feeling after the passing of summer. Fall has times of brilliance, but even though autumn lasts into December on the calendar, its brightness is already gone by now. Summer homes are shuttered and dark and boats that danced on the summer waves now lie lifeless, gathering dust in some storage shed.

Our little lake, frozen over during an early cold spell, has opened up again, but even the moving waves reflect only the gray of cloudy skies. The grasslands still retain a hint of green, but that is nearly obscured by the neutral colors of maturity. Our pines and spruces still hold green needles, giving some life to the landscape. Even these look more nearly black than green under dark clouded skies.

There are some bright contrasts if a person can remember to look for them. Most of the gaily-plumed birds of summer have left the area, but those that remain add a touch of cheer. Few summer birds are as bright as the blue jay and none more friendly than the chickadee. Scarlet-clad deer hunters stand out in the dull woodlands and the fellowship of hunting revives the spirit of many.

Snowmobilers look forward to a few preliminary runs with their machines during early November, and skiers can enjoy the anticipation, if not the practice, of their sport. The latter part of November is cheered by the early snowfall and the feasts and fruitfulness of Thanksgiving.

There is at least one cure for November grayness that always works for me. A good wood fire on the hearth and a glass of tangy apple cider seem to improve the season a great deal. If there's no cider on hand a bowl of popcorn or a crisp apple by the fire seem to do just as well.

Perhaps the grayness of November has some value after all. The dull colors of the natural world create a contrast that makes the bright spots in life seem even more vivid.

Quiet Night

I went for a hike one evening last week, and for the first time in months, hiked by starlight. We often take an evening walk down our country road in both summer and winter. During Daylight Savings Time most of our walks are in daylight or just at sunset. Since our return to Standard Time, every night has been cloudy or rainy; this was our first chance for a starlit walk.

The moon was only a crooked nail paring, hanging low in the southern sky, hardly bright enough to make shadows. The stars did not sparkle with the clear brilliance of a winter evening, but still they were bright and numerous. The Big Dipper was right side up, rather low in the north, and the few other constellations that I know were all visible. The seven tiny stars of the Pleiades were low in the north east, below the flattened "w" of Cassiopia. Orion, the Hunter, with his belt and sword, was lying on the eastern horizon.

The most profound impression, though, was the quietness of the night. When I concentrated on listening , there were some sounds. The breeze rustled in the oak leaves and made a soft sighing in the pines. I could hear the scuffing of my boots as I walked and the soft rhythmic padding of Copper II as he trotted along in the soft sand of the road. Once a small bird fluttered in a roadside tree, and far off I could hear the barking of a dog.

Perhaps the sound I missed the most was the trilling of the tree frogs. They have been going constantly, it seems, since the ice went out last spring. Now we will not hear them again for at least six months. There was a surprising absence of mechanical noise too. The motor bikes and motor boats have come to the end of their season, the winter snarl of snowmobiles has not yet begun, and highway traffic is at a seasonal low. There is always some sound in the world of nature but the aspen leaves have ceased to rattle in the wind, crickets have finished their summer chirping, and not even the hum of a mosquito mars the tranquillity of the night.

This kind of quietness is really refreshing. I believe that one of the serious problems we will have to solve in our struggle to preserve our environment is the problem of noise pollution. Scientific studies have shown that the constant roar of today's mechanized world can, and does, cause serious illness, both physical and mental. We not only need to reduce the noise level in our streets, factories and offices, but we must have noise-free areas to refresh our spirits.

Everyone needs some silence; not absolute silence as in a soundproof room, but relative quiet punctuated by the soothing sounds of nature. Quietness and starlight are the ideal combination!

November, 1985   Prairie Sunsets

We've had some beautiful sunsets during the past week. Every sunset is different, and most are beautiful. The ones we saw in recent days remind me of the prairie sunsets I enjoyed on a camping/goose hunting trip last month.

I drove to the hunting area near Lac Qui Parle Goose Refuge on a Sunday to be ready for hunting early on Monday morning. I was alone on the trip except for Farley, our young golden retriever. I parked our pickup camper near one of the farm buildings, set up camp, and cooked my supper before dark. The trip to the hunting spot had been a long drive, and I felt that a little exercise would be good for both of us.

The gravel road in front of the farm ran east and west; we walked west into the sunset. As soon as we passed the farmstead grove, we were out on the open prairie with nothing to obscure our view of the western sky. The scene was breathtaking! The whole horizon was bright crimson, and the color stretched from north to south. A thin sliver of moon and a single star were visible just above the red glow. As we walked at an easy pace, flock after flock of Canada geese came flying out of the sunset, honking as they passed on their way back to the refuge. I couldn't tell whether Farley appreciated the beauty of the sky, but he was definitely intrigued by the honking of the geese. My own emotions were somewhat mixed: the beauty of the evening was soothing, but at the same time I was filled with excited anticipation by those big game birds.

The next day's hunting turned out to be disappointing. The weather was fair and the geese were flying high. I tried a few long shots, but still had an empty game pocket when the hunting closed for the day at 4 PM. The early closing, however, gave me time to relax for awhile before I fixed my supper. The dishes were washed and there was still time for an evening stroll.

Monday's sunset was beautiful too, but different from that of the evening before. The colors were in pastel shades and not as bright or vibrant. The crescent moon and evening star were a bit higher in the sky. Below them were pink and purple clouds in a pale blue sky with shades of lemon and light orange just above the horizon as the sunset began to fade. There were fewer flocks of geese than we had seen the night before, but enough to renew my optimism for the next day's hunt.

Our home is located in a patch of woods, but we have a fairly open view to the west and southwest. Our sunset colors are just as bright as those on the prairie, but the horizon isn't as wide.

I prefer living in the woodlands where we have some protection from the winter winds, but those prairie sunsets were spectacular!

Let's take time to look at the sky. Not just a casual glance, but a real look. We've seen a few beautiful sunsets and sunrises in recent weeks, but the sky can be beautiful and interesting at any time of day.

Recently I read a short magazine article about an old, abandoned house. It was well written and sort of sad. One phrase in particular caught my attention. It mentioned broken windows looking out on jagged patches of sky that nobody looked at any more. Thinking about that phrase, it seems that hardly anyone watches the sky these days.

Sometimes our attention is caught by a brilliant sunset or the rising, full moon, but mostly we just don't notice the sky. Part of the reason is our increasing urbanization. In some areas the sky is frequently obscured by smog. We don't watch the night sky either; it's hard to see it above the glow of mercury vapor streetlights. Even out in the country, people are more conscious of security lights than they are of Northern Lights.

Most of us don't watch the sky because it really doesn't mean much in our daily lives. We spend most of our time in places that are sheltered from the sky. The weather it brings seldom affects our routine living. There was a time, not so long ago, when most of the people lived closer to the earth. Then everyone was a weather prophet. They judged the coming days by the look of the sky and the feel of the air, and perhaps by the aches in their joints. Mostly though the cloud patterns and wind direction told them what to expect. In those times it was no idle curiosity. Weather changes were vitally important. They determined what the next day's activity would be. Sometimes they determined the crops' profit or loss for the whole year. Farmers and commercial fishermen still watch the sky, but their instincts are supplemented by TV and radio reports.

Some of us who live in the north country still do a bit of sky-watching. We do it mostly on the day before a planned fishing or hunting trip, but most of us have lost the art of doing our own forecasting. In spite of all our complaints and ridicule the professional meteorologist probably does a better job of predicting than any one of us could do. With all the modern equipment the meteorologist is able to "watch" a much larger piece of the sky than we can. Still it seems a shame to have lost the art, for art in any form provides satisfaction to the artist who performs it.

Those of us who live in the north country, especially those who live outside the towns, have some good, clean sky to watch if we are so inclined. Perhaps we could revive the art of sky-watching and get a great deal of pleasure in the process. Maybe we could even learn again to do our own weather forecasting.

Thoughts While Chopping Wood

Much of my hiking time in recent weeks has been devoted to splitting wood. Using an ax in the backyard does not provide as much contact with the world of nature as our usual hikes, but it is a good healthy outdoor activity that allows some time for thinking.

We have recently bucked up part of the wood I cut last winter. Most of the largest logs were split when the trees were felled. In midwinter, when the wood is frozen, a few blows with a light ax are sufficient to split a good-sized log. The split logs are easier to handle and also dry better during the summer. There are always a few pieces with knots that can't be split until they are cut into shorter lengths. These I am splitting now before storing them away.

There is a certain joy in working with wood. I notice it more when doing carpentry or wood finishing, but some of the same feeling is here in the rough chunks of firewood. It's not just the beauty of the grain nor the clean odor of new wood, though these are pleasant. There is a sort of fundamental honesty about wood. Its weight and strength are a constant factor and one knows instinctively that a piece of wood will do the job for which it is being prepared. There is no concern about shoddy work or faulty engineering as there is with many man-made products. Oak always reacts like oak and birch always looks like birch. The woodsman knows the constant properties of each and finds satisfaction in that knowledge.

There is a joy in the work as well as in the wood. Splitting firewood isn't a complex job, but there is a certain amount of skill involved in handling an ax. Some judgment is required to select the easiest way to split each block. Both the skill and the judgment soon become subconscious.

Cutting wood is good exercise. It's strenuous enough so that an occasional rest is in order. Usually there are no deadlines to meet so the work doesn't need to be rushed. Those short breathers are a good time to sit on a wood block and absorb the atmosphere—to watch the migrating birds and wonder where they will spend the winter and how soon they will return; to watch reflections in the still lake waters and feel the openness of the horizon now that summer foliage no longer obscures the view.

We never seem to quite finish the wood cutting at our house. There always seems to be other, more demanding, jobs to be done. We always seem to get enough wood stored away to provide dry fuel so that we can feel somewhat prepared for another north country winter.

One day last week our daughter Carla and I, along with Farley, our Golden Retriever, went for a hike on the south forty. We were checking the condition of my deer-hunting stands and ended up studying some interesting shrubs.

We had found the newest stand in good condition and were moving on when Carla stopped to examine a gnarly-looking bush. "That's a thorn apple," I said, pointing out the one-and-a-half inch, needle-sharp thorns on the branches. I recalled that, as a boy, I tried to eat the "apples," which were little more than skin and seeds.

Down by the old stock-watering pit we came upon a bramble patch of these same plants. Here some of the dried out red "apples" still remained on the small trees. I picked a few and offered them to Farley who accepted them, but then dropped them on the ground. Apparently they were too hard for the dog to chew. This surprised me because Farley is quite fond of rose hips, which these fruits resemble.

Farley's appetite for rose hips started several years ago. I was picking wild raspberries and offered a few to the dog. He ate them with apparent relish and waited for more. I showed him how to pick his own berries and have since wondered if this was such a good thing to have done. The berry season lasts only a few weeks but the dog discovered that rose hips were edible well into the winter. Rose hips are said to be a good source of vitamin C, so I suspect they are good for the dog.

Back at the house I got out my old botany textbook to see what information I could glean about thorn apples. To my surprise there was no such name in the book. I had no leaves or flowers to use in keying on the plant type, and have almost forgotten how to use a plant species key. After reading extensively and looking at pictures I concluded that my "thorn apple" was really hawthorn. The fruits that I called apples were called "haws." This makes the name hawthorn quite appropriate; these shrubs produce a good crop of haws and the thorns are hard to ignore!

Using my jackknife I opened several of these haws. I found that they were very thin-skinned and each contained four very hard seeds. The book referred to these fruits as nutlets. I picked a couple of rose hips that the dog had not yet found and opened them for comparison. Rose hips had a bit of flesh under the skin and were filled with a few dozen much smaller seeds. I could see why the dog preferred these over the haws. Both of these plants belong to the family Rosaceae (the rose family). This is a very large group which includes roses, apples, and a great many other plants.

It seems as though there is always something to learn in the world of nature. None of us will ever learn it all. Still the great variety of plants and animals that surround us add spice to our lives!

Gratitude

As we hike down the road into the coming winter, let's ponder a few reasons for giving thanks. It's impossible to list all our reasons for gratitude. Such a list would be so lengthy that it would serve no purpose. Perhaps we could consider the things that mean most to each of us. Such an exercise may help develop the feeling of reverent contentment that is the essence of thanksgiving.

We tend to take for granted the really basic necessities of living, such as air, water, food, shelter and clothing. In addition our generation has a whole list of newer "necessities" that we consider only on rare occasions; plumbing, central heating, transportation, radio and TV entertainment are considered an everyday part of modern living. A few generations ago such things were undreamed of luxuries.

In contrast to these new conveniences, there is a group of things that are very old but, like antiques, are becoming more precious because of their scarcity, like clean air, pure water, and unspoiled wilderness— more rare with each year that our population grows. I am particularly thankful that I live in an area where there are still secluded places I can go when I feel the need for solitude. There are few places left on earth like this and only a small part of the world's population has this privilege.

Some of the things that make life most worthwhile are quite mundane—little things that we notice during their seasons and then forget until the calendar brings them around again for our renewed enjoyment. I am always pleased by the rumbling of the first thunderstorm and the spring rains that follow. The sparkle of sunlight on the water after the ice has melted fills me with joy, as does the sound of grouse drumming in the spring woods. I'm grateful for the warmth of summer sun, the sound of the catbird's song and the smell of wild roses and new-mown hay.

The beauty of the autumn woodland is a glory we can never forget, and yet each fall it seems as though it could never have been this lovely before. Winter has its glory too, in the shining expanses of newly formed ice and the snow powder on evergreen boughs. This season brings a new appreciation of family and friends also as we gather for holiday celebrations.

All through the year these little things add to the joy of living, reminding me often of the following lines from Robert Louis Stevenson: "The world is so full of a number of things, I'm sure we should all be as happy as kings."

Our hike today may contain more philosophy than nature. Most nature lovers are philosophers as well, so perhaps these words won't prove too hard to take. Along with wandering from our usual field of observation I am going to steal someone else's ideas, but knowing the writer, I don't think he will mind too much.

In a recent issue of The Country Echo Craig Nagel had an excellent article on why men hunt. Craig did a good job of saying things that many of us find hard to express; he also threw in some excellent philosophy. He quoted extensively from Thoreau on the desperation of men's lives and closed the article with a profound statement of his own. His final sentence had occupied my thoughts for several days. It read, "For a brief while life becomes, not a problem to be solved, but a mystery to be lived."

I wonder if this bit of wisdom cannot be expanded to include a great deal more of life than hunting. Through the years a number of my friends and I have spent a lot of time and mental energy—and a bit of agony, too—pondering the meaning of life. We considered it to be a riddle that had to be figured out if life was to be satisfying. During the past few years this problem hasn't seemed quite so important, but still I had the vague feeling that I was neglecting my mental work when I wasn't searching for a solution. I find it rather refreshing to consider the possibility that life isn't really a problem and therefore a solution isn't necessary.

Now instead of worrying about things that I can't figure out, I can enjoy them without trying to analyze them. Such a philosophy can change a person's whole outlook. The "daily grind" of employment may still be a grind, but it seems less burdensome if we approach each day as a "mystery to be lived."

In the world of nature we need no longer try to understand why summer must end or autumn leaves must fall or sunsets must disappear. Instead of searching for answers we can spend our energies discovering the beauty and perfection in every day's mystery. We aren't compelled to find the meaning in birth and growth and death in the natural world. We can let the seasons roll on as they always have and just marvel at the beauty of it all. Viewing life as a mystery to be lived rather than a problem to be solved seems an ideal sort of philosophy.